Biscuits

THE AUSTRALIAN
Women's Weekly

Biscuits

Macquarie
Regional Library

CONTENTS

Biscuit-making is easy, and what's more, you as the baker, know exactly what ingredients have gone into the recipe. Here are some tips to help you produce wonderful biscuits.

Measuring Ingredients should be weighed and measured carefully. Don't overbeat butter, sugar and egg mixtures, beat them until they're combined. Don't over-grease oven trays, this will make the bottoms of the biscuits burn; baking paper can be used for all biscuit baking. Oven trays should have tiny sides to allow the oven to bake and brown biscuits evenly.

When are they cooked? With the exception of meringues, macaroons and biscotti, most baked biscuits and slices should feel slightly soft when they're done; they become crisp as they cool.

Cooling Biscuits should be cooled either on oven trays or wire racks.

Storing Plain unfilled, un-iced biscuits, slices, meringues and macaroons will keep well in an airtight container, with as little air space around them as possible, at room temperature, for up to four days. Biscotti will keep this way for at least a month. If biscuits soften during storage, place them in a single layer on an oven tray, re-crisp them in 180°C/160°C fan-forced for about 5 minutes. All of these plain biscuits can be frozen for a month or more, there's no point in freezing biscotti.

Iced and/or filled biscuits and slices, are usually best kept in the fridge for up to about four days. They can be frozen, but often the icing will look a bit sad after thawing. Keep no-bake biscuits in the fridge.

Now go and have some fun – bake a batch of biscuits.

SAVOURY BISCUITS

blue cheese twists

1¼ cups (185g) plain flour
¼ cup (35g) self-raising flour
½ teaspoon salt
60g butter, chopped finely
125g firm blue vein cheese, grated
½ cup (160g) grated tasty cheese
1 egg yolk
3 teaspoons water, approximately
pinch paprika

1 Sift flours and salt into large bowl; rub in butter. Stir in cheeses.
Add egg yolk and enough water to make a firm dough. Knead dough
gently on floured surface until smooth. Cover; refrigerate 30 minutes.
2 Preheat oven to 180°C/160°C fan-forced. Grease oven trays.
3 Roll dough between sheets of baking paper into a rectangle about
3mm thick. Cut into 1cm x 10cm strips. Twist each strip, place about
2cm apart on oven trays; sprinkle strips lightly with paprika.
4 Bake twists about 20 minutes or until lightly browned. Cool on trays.

prep + cook time 50 minutes (+ refrigeration) **makes** 80

curry caraway crackers

1 tablespoon curry powder
1¼ cups (185g) plain flour
¼ cup (35g) self-raising flour
100g butter, chopped finely
1 egg, beaten lightly
1 teaspoon water, approximately
1 egg white, beaten lightly
1 teaspoon sea salt
½ teaspoon caraway seeds

1 Dry-fry curry powder in small frying pan over low heat until fragrant. Cool.
2 Sift flours and curry powder into large bowl; rub in butter. Stir in whole egg and enough water to make a firm dough. Knead dough on floured surface until smooth. Cover; refrigerate 30 minutes.
3 Preheat oven to 180°C/160°C fan-forced. Grease oven trays.
4 Roll dough between sheets of baking paper to 2mm thickness. Cut into 5cm rounds; place about 3cm apart onto oven trays. Brush lightly with a little egg white; sprinkle with salt and caraway seeds.
5 Bake crackers about 12 minutes or until lightly browned. Cool on trays.

prep + cook time 40 minutes (+ refrigeration) **makes** 70

oat cakes with cheddar and fig jam

1 cup (90g) rolled oats
100g cold butter, chopped coarsely
½ cup (75g) wholemeal plain flour
2 tablespoons plain flour
¼ teaspoon bicarbonate of soda
1½ tablespoons brown sugar
1 tablespoon milk
200g cheddar cheese
1 cup (320g) fig jam

1 Preheat oven to 160°C/140°C fan-forced. Grease oven trays.
2 Process oats until chopped finely. Add butter and sifted dry ingredients; pulse until crumbly. Add milk; process until mixture comes together. Knead dough gently on floured surface until smooth.
3 Divide dough in half; roll each half between sheets of baking paper until 3mm thick. Cut dough into 3cm squares. Using spatula, carefully place oat cakes on trays.
4 Bake oat cakes 15 minutes or until golden brown. Cool oat cakes on trays 5 minutes; transfer to wire racks to cool completely. Serve oat cakes topped with a small piece of cheese and a little jam.

prep + cook time 40 minutes **makes** 80

tomato basil crackers

1¼ cups (185g) plain flour
30g butter, chopped finely
2 tablespoons chopped fresh basil
2 tablespoons tomato paste
¼ teaspoon ground black pepper
2 tablespoons water, approximately
1 egg white, beaten lightly
2 teaspoons sea salt

1 Sift flour into large bowl; rub in butter. Stir in basil, paste and pepper; add enough water to mix to a firm dough. Knead dough on floured surface until smooth. Cover; refrigerate 30 minutes.
2 Preheat oven to 180°C/160°C fan-forced. Grease oven trays.
3 Roll dough on floured surface until 2mm thick. Prick all over with fork; cut into 4cm squares. Place about 1cm apart on trays. Brush with a little egg white; sprinkle with a little salt.
4 Bake crackers about 15 minutes or until lightly browned; cool on trays.

prep + cook time 40 minutes (+ refrigeration) **makes** 60

herb and garlic triangles

1 cup (150g) plain flour
½ teaspoon dry mustard
½ teaspoon garlic powder
100g butter, chopped finely
1 tablespoon finely chopped fresh flat-leaf parsley
1 tablespoon finely chopped fresh basil leaves
1 tablespoon finely chopped fresh chives
½ cup (60g) grated cheddar cheese
1 egg yolk

1 Sift dry ingredients into large bowl; rub in butter. Stir in herbs, cheese and egg yolk. Knead dough gently on floured surface until smooth. Cover; refrigerate 30 minutes.
2 Preheat oven to 200°C/180°C fan-forced. Grease oven trays.
3 Roll dough between sheets of baking paper to 3mm thickness. Cut dough into 4cm squares; cut squares into triangles. Place about 1cm apart on trays.
4 Bake triangles about 10 minutes or until lightly browned; cool on trays.

prep + cook time 40 minutes (+ refrigeration) **makes** 80

poppy seed pretzels

1⅔ cups (250g) plain flour
2 teaspoons lemon juice
⅔ cup (160ml) water, approximately
200g butter, softened
1 egg, beaten lightly
3 teaspoons poppy seeds
1 teaspoon paprika
pinch cayenne pepper
2 tablespoons finely grated parmesan cheese
1 teaspoon salt

1 Sift flour into large bowl. Add juice and enough water to mix to a sticky dough. Knead on floured surface about 5 minutes or until smooth. Cover; refrigerate 15 minutes.
2 Place dough on floured surface; cut a 2cm-deep cross into surface of dough. Pull corners of dough out to form a four-leaf clover shape, about 36cm square.
3 Shape butter into 12cm square; place butter on centre of dough. Fold flaps over each other to encase butter; roll 20cm x 40cm. Fold over bottom third of dough, fold top third over bottom third. Cover; refrigerate 10 minutes.
4 Preheat oven to 220°C/200°C fan-forced. Grease oven trays.
5 Repeat rolling, folding and resting of dough three times, half turning the dough before rolling. Roll dough into 20cm x 40cm rectangle; fold both ends over to meet in centre. Fold dough in half; cover, refrigerate 10 minutes. Repeat process.
6 Roll dough on floured surface until 4mm thick. Brush with egg; sprinkle with half the seeds, then paprika, pepper and cheese. Cut into 1cm x 15cm strips.
7 Twist strips into pretzels and twists. Brush uncut surfaces with egg; sprinkle with remaining seeds and salt. Place 4cm apart on trays. Bake about 10 minutes or until lightly browned and crisp.

prep + cook time 50 minutes (+ refrigeration) **makes** 60

parmesan scones with goat's cheese and tapenade

1½ cups (225g) self-raising flour
30g butter
¼ cup (30g) finely grated parmesan cheese
¾ cup (180ml) buttermilk, approximately
180g goat's cheese
bunch fresh flat-leaf parsley
tapenade
200g seeded black olives
1 tablespoon rinsed drained capers
1 clove garlic, quartered
½ cup coarsely chopped fresh flat-leaf parsley
5 drained anchovy fillets
1 tablespoon lemon juice
1 tablespoon olive oil

1 Preheat oven to 200°C/180°C fan-forced. Grease oven tray.
2 Sift flour into large bowl; rub in butter, then stir in parmesan. Using a knife, mix in enough buttermilk to make a soft dough. Knead dough gently on floured surface until smooth.
3 Press dough out to 1.5cm thickness, cut out 30 x 3cm rounds. Place scones, barely touching each other, on tray.
4 Bake scones about 20 minutes. Turn onto wire rack; cover, cool.
5 Meanwhile, make tapenade.
6 Split scones in half, top each half with tapenade and goat's cheese; top each with a parsley leaf.
tapenade Process ingredients until chopped coarsely.

prep + cook time 45 minutes **makes** 60
tip Good quality tapenade is easy to buy if you don't want to make your own.

fennel grissini with prosciutto

2 cups (300g) plain flour
½ teaspoon white sugar
1 teaspoon cooking salt
1 teaspoon dried yeast
2 teaspoons fennel seeds
1 cup (250ml) water, approximately
cooking-oil spray
sea salt
20 slices prosciutto (300g)

1 Sift flour, sugar and cooking salt into medium bowl, stir in yeast, seeds and enough of the water to make a soft dough. Knead dough on floured surface about 5 minutes or until smooth and elastic.
2 Place dough in large oiled bowl, cover with plastic wrap; stand in warm place about 1 hour or until dough is doubled in size.
3 Preheat oven to 220°C/200°C fan-forced. Grease oven trays.
4 Turn dough onto floured surface, knead until smooth. Divide dough into four portions, cut each portion into 15 pieces; roll each piece into a long thin stick. Place sticks on oven trays, coat lightly with cooking oil spray. Sprinkle with sea salt.
5 Bake grissini about 15 minutes or until crisp.
6 Meanwhile, cut each prosciutto slice lengthways into three. Wrap a strip around each warm grissini. Serve immediately.

prep + cook time 1 hour (+ standing) **makes** 60

vegemite cheese straws

2 sheets puff pastry
1 tablespoon vegemite
⅔ cup (50g) finely grated parmesan cheese

1 Preheat oven to 220°C/200°C fan-forced. Grease oven trays;
line with baking paper.
2 Spread one pastry sheet with half the vegemite; sprinkle with
half the cheese. Top with remaining pastry sheet; spread with
remaining vegemite, then sprinkle with remaining cheese.
3 Cut pastry stack in half; place one stack on top of the other, press
down firmly. Cut pastry crossways into 24 strips; twist each strip,
pinching ends to seal. Place on trays.
4 Bake straws about 12 minutes or until browned lightly.

prep + cook time 30 minutes **makes** 24

spinach and fetta pinwheels

250g frozen spinach, thawed
100g fetta cheese, crumbled
½ cup (40g) finely grated parmesan cheese
2 sheets puff pastry
1 egg

1 Preheat oven to 220°C/200°C fan-forced. Grease oven trays;
line with baking paper.
2 Squeeze excess moisture from spinach. Chop spinach coarsely;
pat dry between sheets of absorbent paper.
3 Sprinkle spinach and combined cheeses over pastry sheets. Roll
pastry tightly to enclose filling. Cut each roll into 12 slices. Place
pinwheels, cut-side up, on trays; brush with a little egg.
4 Bake pinwheels about 15 minutes or until browned lightly.

prep + cook time 30 minutes **makes** 24

PLAIN BISCUITS

gingernuts

90g butter
1/3 cup (75g) firmly packed brown sugar
1/3 cup (115g) golden syrup
1 1/3 cups (200g) plain flour
3/4 teaspoon bicarbonate of soda
1 tablespoon ground ginger
1 teaspoon ground cinnamon
1/4 teaspoon ground clove

1 Preheat oven to 180°C/160°C fan-forced. Grease oven trays.
2 Stir butter, sugar and syrup in medium saucepan over low heat until smooth. Remove from heat; stir in sifted dry ingredients. Cool 10 minutes.
3 Roll rounded teaspoons of mixture into balls. Place balls about 3cm apart on trays; flatten slightly.
4 Bake gingernuts about 10 minutes; cool on trays.

prep + cook time 25 minutes (+ cooling) **makes** 32

peanut butter cookies

125g butter, softened
¼ cup (70g) crunchy peanut butter
¾ cup (165g) firmly packed brown sugar
1 egg
1½ cups (225g) plain flour
½ teaspoon bicarbonate of soda
½ cup (70g) roasted unsalted peanuts, chopped coarsely

1 Preheat oven to 180°C/160°C fan-forced. Grease oven trays;
line with baking paper.
2 Beat butter, peanut butter, sugar and egg in small bowl with electric
mixer until smooth; do not overmix. Transfer mixture to medium bowl;
stir in sifted flour and soda, then nuts.
3 Roll level tablespoons of mixture into balls; place 5cm apart on trays,
flatten with floured fork.
4 Bake cookies about 12 minutes; cool on trays.

prep + cook time 25 minutes **makes** 30

dutch ginger biscuits

250g butter, softened
¾ cup (165g) firmly packed brown sugar
1 egg
2 cups (300g) plain flour
1 teaspoon ground ginger
⅓ cup (60g) finely chopped glacé ginger

1 Preheat oven to 180°C/160°C fan-forced. Grease oven trays; line with baking paper.
2 Beat butter, sugar and egg in small bowl with electric mixer until combined. Stir in sifted flour and ground ginger, in two batches. Stir in glacé ginger.
3 Roll level tablespoons of dough into balls; place about 3cm apart on trays, flatten with fork.
4 Bake biscuits about 15 minutes; cool on trays.

prep + cook time 35 minutes **makes** 36

madeleines

2 eggs
2 tablespoons caster sugar
2 tablespoons icing sugar
¼ cup (35g) self-raising flour
¼ cup (35g) plain flour
75g unsalted butter, melted
1 tablespoon water
2 tablespoons icing sugar, extra

1 Preheat oven to 200°C/180°C fan-forced. Grease two 12-hole
(1½-tablespoon/30ml) madeleine pans.
2 Beat eggs and sifted sugars in small bowl with electric mixer until thick
and creamy.
3 Meanwhile, triple-sift flours; sift flour over egg mixture. Pour combined
butter and the water down side of bowl then fold ingredients together.
4 Drop rounded tablespoons of mixture into each pan hole. Bake about
10 minutes. Tap hot pan firmly on bench to release madeleines then turn,
top-side down, onto wire rack to cool. Serve dusted with sifted extra icing
sugar.

variation
orange madeleines Add 1 teaspoon finely grated orange rind when
beating the egg mixture. Omit the water and replace with 1 tablespoon
orange juice.

prep + cook time 25 minutes **makes** 24

chocolate shortbread stars

250g unsalted butter, softened
1 cup (160g) icing sugar
1¼ cups (185g) plain flour
½ cup (100g) rice flour
¼ cup (25g) cocoa powder
60g (125) dark Choc Bits
2 tablespoons icing sugar, extra

1 Beat butter and sugar in medium bowl with electric mixer until light
and fluffy. Stir in sifted flours and cocoa, in two batches. Knead on
floured surface until smooth. Roll dough between sheets of baking
paper until 1cm thick. Refrigerate 30 minutes.
2 Preheat oven to 160°C/140°C fan-forced. Grease two oven trays;
line with baking paper.
3 Cut 25 x 6.5cm stars from dough. Place stars about 4cm apart on
trays; decorate with Choc Bits.
4 Bake stars about 20 minutes; cool on trays. Dust stars with extra
sifted icing sugar.

prep + cook time 45 minutes (+ refrigeration) **makes** 24

choc-vanilla spiral cookies

200g butter, softened
⅔ cup (150g) caster sugar
1 teaspoon vanilla extract
1 egg
2½ cups (375g) plain flour
1 tablespoon cocoa powder

1 Beat butter, sugar, extract and egg in small bowl with electric mixer until light and fluffy. Divide mixture between two medium bowls; stir half the sifted flour into one bowl, mix to form a firm dough. Stir remaining sifted flour and cocoa into second bowl, mix to form a firm dough. Knead each piece of dough, separately, on a floured surface until smooth. Cover; refrigerate 30 minutes.
2 Roll vanilla dough between sheets of baking paper into a 25cm x 35cm rectangle; repeat with chocolate dough. Remove top sheet of paper from each dough. Turn vanilla dough onto chocolate dough, remove top sheet of paper; trim edges. Using bottom sheet of paper as a guide, roll dough stack tightly from long side. Enclose roll in plastic wrap; refrigerate 30 minutes.
3 Preheat oven to 180°C/160°C fan-forced. Grease oven trays; line with baking paper.
4 Remove plastic from roll; cut roll into 1cm slices. Place slices about 2cm apart on trays.
5 Bake cookies about 15 minutes. Stand cookies on trays 5 minutes; transfer to wire rack to cool.

prep + cook time 45 minutes (+ refrigeration) **makes** 28

scorched peanut cookies

125g butter, chopped
¼ cup (70g) crunchy peanut butter
¾ cup (150g) firmly packed brown sugar
1 egg
1½ cups (225g) plain flour
½ teaspoon bicarbonate of soda
¾ cup (100g) scorched peanuts

1 Preheat oven to 180°C/160°C fan-forced. Grease oven trays.
2 Beat butter, peanut butter, sugar and egg in small bowl with electric mixer until well combined. Transfer mixture to large bowl; stir in sifted dry ingredients and nuts.
3 Roll rounded teaspoons of mixture into balls with floured hands. Place about 3cm apart on trays; flatten slightly with hand.
4 Bake cookies about 12 minutes or until lightly browned; cool on trays.

prep + cook time 30 minutes **makes** 50
tip Scorched peanuts are chocolate-coated peanuts, and are available in most supermarkets.

golden cinnamon biscuits

60g butter
⅓ cup (115g) golden syrup
2 tablespoons brown sugar
2 tablespoons caster sugar
1¼ cups (185g) self-raising flour
3 teaspoons ground cinnamon

1 Preheat oven to 200°C/180°C fan-forced. Grease oven trays.
2 Stir butter, golden syrup and sugars in medium heavy-based saucepan over low heat until butter is melted; cool 5 minutes. Stir in flour and cinnamon.
3 Roll rounded teaspoons of mixture into balls, place about 2cm apart on trays; flatten with a floured fork until 1cm thick.
4 Bake biscuits about 10 minutes or until browned. Stand biscuits on trays 5 minutes; transfer to wire racks to cool.

prep + cook time 35 minutes **makes** 30

cream cheese, coconut and lime cookies

250g butter, softened
90g soft cream cheese
1 tablespoon finely grated lime rind
1 cup (220g) firmly packed brown sugar
2 eggs
1¼ cups (185g) plain flour
1 cup (150g) self-raising flour
½ cup (40g) desiccated coconut

1 Preheat oven to 180°C/160°C fan-forced. Grease oven trays;
line with baking paper.
2 Beat butter, cream cheese, rind and sugar in small bowl with electric
mixer until light and fluffy. Beat in eggs, one at a time. Transfer mixture
to large bowl; stir in sifted flours and coconut, in two batches.
3 Roll level tablespoons of dough into balls, place about 3cm apart on
trays; flatten slightly.
4 Bake cookies about 15 minutes; cool on trays.

prep + cook time 40 minutes **makes** 36

lemon shortbread stars

125g unsalted butter, softened
2 teaspoons finely grated lemon rind
2 tablespoons caster sugar
1cup (150g) plain flour
2 tablespoons rice flour
1 tablespoon demerara sugar

1 Preheat oven to 160°C/140°C fan-forced. Grease two oven trays;
line with baking paper.
2 Beat butter, rind and caster sugar in medium bowl with electric mixer
until light and fluffy. Stir in sifted flours, in two batches. Knead on floured
surface until smooth. Roll dough between sheets of baking paper until
5mm thick. Refrigerate 30 minutes.
3 Cut 15 x 5cm stars from dough. Place stars about 4cm apart on trays;
sprinkle with demerara sugar.
4 Bake stars about 15 minutes; cool on trays.

prep + cook time 45 minutes (+ refrigeration) **makes** 15

chocolate hazelnut thins

1 egg white
¼ cup (55g) brown sugar
2 tablespoons plain flour
2 teaspoons cocoa powder
30g butter, melted
1 teaspoon milk
1 tablespoon ground hazelnuts

1 Preheat oven to 180°C/160°C fan-forced. Grease oven trays.
2 Beat egg white in small bowl with electric mixer until soft peaks form; gradually add sugar, beating until sugar dissolves. Stir in sifted flour and cocoa, then butter, milk and ground hazelnuts.
3 Spread level teaspoons of mixture into 8cm circles, about 4cm apart on trays.
4 Bake thins, in batches, about 5 minutes. Remove from tray immediately using metal spatula, place over rolling pin to cool.

prep + cook time 25 minutes **makes** 24

black sugar and ginger snaps

1 cup (200g) firmly packed black sugar
3 teaspoons ground ginger
2 tablespoons finely chopped glacé ginger
2 cups (300g) plain flour
200g butter, chopped
1 egg

1 Preheat oven to 160°C/140°C fan-forced. Grease oven trays.
2 Process sugar, gingers, flour and butter until mixture resembles breadcrumbs. Add egg; process until mixture forms a ball. Knead dough on floured surface until smooth.
3 Roll rounded teaspoons of mixture into balls, place about 5cm apart on trays; flatten slightly with a floured fork.
4 Bake biscuits about 25 minutes or until browned. Stand biscuits on trays 5 minutes; transfer to wire racks to cool.

prep + cook time 45 minutes **makes** 60
tip Black sugar is available from health food stores; brown sugar can be used as a substitute.

greek almond biscuits

3 cups (375g) ground almonds
1 cup (220g) caster sugar
3 drops almond essence
3 egg whites, beaten lightly
1 cup (80g) flaked almonds

1 Preheat oven to 180°C/160°C fan-forced. Grease oven trays;
line baking trays.
2 Combine ground almonds, sugar and essence in large bowl. Stir in
egg white until mixture forms a firm paste.
3 Roll level tablespoons of mixture in flaked almonds; roll into 8cm logs.
Press on remaining almonds. Shape logs into crescents; place on trays.
4 Bake biscuits about 15 minutes or until browned lightly; cool on trays.

prep + cook time 45 minutes (+ cooling) **makes** 25

coconut fortune cookies

2 egg whites
⅓ cup (55g) icing sugar
1 teaspoon coconut essence
30g butter, melted
⅓ cup (50g) plain flour
¼ cup (20g) desiccated coconut, toasted

1 Prepare small slips of paper with "fortunes".
2 Preheat oven to 180°C/160°C fan-forced. Grease and flour oven trays; mark two 8cm circles on each tray.
3 Beat egg whites in small bowl with electric mixer until just foamy; gradually beat in sifted icing sugar, essence and butter. Stir in sifted flour until smooth.
4 Place a level teaspoon of mixture in centre of each marked circle on trays, spread evenly to cover circle completely; sprinkle evenly with a little coconut.
5 Bake, one tray at a time, about 5 minutes or until lightly browned around the edges; remove from oven. Working quickly, place one slip of paper on each cookie, then lift cookies from tray, fold in half, then lightly bend cookies over the rim of a glass; cool 30 seconds. Place cookies on wire rack to cool completely. Repeat with remaining cookie mixture and coconut.

prep + cook time 45 minutes (+ cooling) **makes** 45

sugar and spice shortbread

500g butter, softened
1 cup (220g) caster sugar
4½ cups (675g) plain flour
½ cup (75g) rice flour
1 teaspoon mixed spice
36 whole cloves
2 tablespoons white sugar

1 Beat butter and caster sugar in large bowl with electric mixer until light and fluffy. Stir in flours and spice; press mixture together with hands to form a firm dough. Knead gently on floured surface until smooth. Divide dough in half; cover halves, refrigerate 30 minutes.
2 Preheat oven to 150°C/130°C fan-forced. Grease oven trays.
3 Working with one half of dough at a time, roll dough between sheets of baking paper until 1cm thick. Cut dough into 6cm-fluted rounds using a cutter. Re-roll scraps.
4 Place rounds about 3cm apart on trays, decorate with cloves; sprinkle with white sugar.
5 Bake shortbread about 30 minutes or until a pale-straw colour. Stand shortbread on trays 5 minutes; transfer to wire racks to cool.

prep + cook time 50 minutes (+ refrigeration) **makes** 36

pecan choc-chunk cookies

You will need to process about 1 cup (120g) pecans for the amount of ground pecans in this recipe.

125g butter, softened
¼ cup (55g) caster sugar
¼ cup (55g) firmly packed brown sugar
1 egg
1 cup (150g) plain flour
¾ cup (90g) ground pecans
150g milk eating chocolate, chopped coarsely
½ cup (60g) coarsely chopped pecans

1 Preheat oven to 180°C/160°C fan-forced. Grease oven trays; line with baking paper.
2 Beat butter, sugars and egg in small bowl with electric mixer until combined. Stir in sifted flour, then ground pecans, chocolate and nuts.
3 Drop level tablespoons of mixture about 5cm apart on trays; flatten slightly.
4 Bake cookies about 15 minutes; cool on trays.

prep + cook time 30 minutes **makes** 28

sticky date cookies

1 cup (140g) coarsely chopped seeded dates
2 tablespoons golden syrup
2 tablespoons water
¼ teaspoon bicarbonate of soda
1 teaspoon finely grated orange rind
1¾ cups (255g) plain flour
¾ cup (165g) caster sugar
100g butter, chopped coarsely
1 egg
¼ cup (40g) icing sugar

1 Preheat oven to 180°C/160°C fan-forced. Grease two oven trays; line with baking paper.
2 Bring dates, syrup and the water to the boil in small saucepan. Remove from heat, stir in soda and rind; stand 5 minutes. Process mixture until almost smooth; cool.
3 Add flour, caster sugar, butter and egg to processor; process until ingredients come together. Refrigerate mixture 30 minutes.
4 Roll heaped teaspoons of mixture into balls; flatten slightly. Place about 3cm apart on oven trays.
5 Bake cookies about 15 minutes; cool on trays. Toss cookies in sifted icing sugar.

prep + cook time 45 minutes (+ refrigeration) **makes** 30

orange polenta biscuits

250g butter, softened
1 teaspoon vanilla extract
1¼ cups (200g) icing sugar
3 tablespoons finely grated orange rind
½ cup (85g) polenta
2½ cups (375g) plain flour
1 tablespoon orange juice

1 Beat butter, extract, sugar and 1 teaspoon of the rind in small bowl with electric mixer until combined. Stir in polenta, then flour and juice, in two batches. Knead dough on floured surface until smooth.
2 Divide dough in half; shape into two 20cm triangular logs. Cover; refrigerate 2 hours or until firm.
3 Preheat oven to 200°C/180°C fan-forced. Grease oven trays.
4 Cut logs into 1cm slices. Place triangles about 2cm apart on trays; sprinkle with remaining orange rind.
5 Bake biscuits about 15 minutes or until browned lightly. Stand biscuits on trays 5 minutes; transfer to wire racks to cool.

prep + cook time 45 minutes (+ refrigeration) **makes** 40

chewy chocolate caramel cookies

125g butter, softened
½ cup (110g) caster sugar
1 egg
1 cup (150g) plain flour
2 tablespoons cocoa powder
2 x 60g Chokito bars, chopped finely

1 Preheat oven to 180°C/160°C fan-forced. Grease oven trays;
line with baking paper.
2 Beat butter, sugar and egg in small bowl with electric mixer until
smooth; do not overbeat. Transfer mixture to medium bowl; stir in sifted
flour and cocoa, then chopped chocolate bar.
3 Drop level tablespoons of mixture about 5cm apart onto trays.
4 Bake cookies about 15 minutes; cool on trays.

prep + cook time 25 minutes **makes** 24
tip Chokito bars are chocolate-coated caramel fudge bars with
crunchy rice crisps. They are available from supermarkets and
confectionery stores.

sugar and spice snaps

1½ cups (225g) plain flour
¾ cup (165g) firmly packed dark muscovado sugar
2 teaspoons ground ginger
1 teaspoon mixed spice
¼ teaspoon ground clove
150g butter, chopped coarsely
1 egg yolk
¼ cup (55g) raw sugar

1 Process flour, muscovado sugar, spices and butter until crumbly. Add egg yolk; process until combined. Knead dough on floured surface until smooth. Cover; refrigerate 30 minutes.
2 Divide dough in half; roll each half between sheets of baking paper to 3mm thickness. Refrigerate 30 minutes.
3 Preheat oven to 180°C/160°C fan-forced. Line three oven trays with baking paper.
4 Cut thirty 7cm rounds from dough. Place rounds on trays; sprinkle with raw sugar.
5 Bake snaps about 10 minutes; cool on trays.

prep + cook time 45 minutes (+ refrigeration) **makes** 30

choc-cherry bliss bombs

1 ⅓ cups (200g) milk chocolate Melts
60g butter
¼ cup (60ml) vegetable oil
⅓ cup (75g) caster sugar
2 eggs
1 cup (150g) self-raising flour
1 cup (150g) plain flour
3 x 55g Cherry Ripe bars, chopped finely
¼ cup (20g) desiccated coconut

1 Stir chocolate, butter, oil and sugar in medium saucepan over low heat until smooth. Cool 15 minutes.
2 Preheat oven to 180°C/160°C fan-forced. Grease oven trays; line with baking paper.
3 Stir eggs and flours into chocolate mixture; stir in Cherry Ripe.
4 Roll level ½ teaspoons of mixture into balls; roll half the balls in coconut. Place about 2cm apart on oven trays.
5 Bake cookies about 10 minutes; cool on trays.

prep + cook time 40 minutes **makes** 280
tips Cherry Ripe bars are chocolate-coated cherry and coconut bars. They are available from supermarkets and confectionery stores. Remember, these cookies are bite-sized so this recipe will make a few hundred bliss bombs.

wholemeal rosemary butter rounds

125g butter, softened
2 teaspoons finely grated orange rind
1 cup (220g) firmly packed brown sugar
1⅓ cups (200g) wholemeal self-raising flour
1 cup (100g) walnuts, roasted, chopped coarsely
⅔ cup (100g) raisins, halved
2 teaspoons dried rosemary
⅓ cup (80ml) orange juice
⅔ cup (50g) desiccated coconut
⅔ cup (60g) rolled oats

1 Preheat oven to 180°C/160°C fan-forced. Grease oven trays; line with baking paper.
2 Beat butter, rind and sugar in small bowl with electric mixer until combined. Transfer mixture to medium bowl; stir in flour then remaining ingredients.
3 Roll rounded tablespoons of mixture into balls, place about 5cm apart on oven trays; flatten slightly.
4 Bake biscuits about 15 minutes; cool on trays.

prep + cook time 30 minutes **makes** 28

double choc-chip chilli cookies

250g butter, softened
1 teaspoon vanilla extract
¾ cup (165g) caster sugar
¾ cup (165g) firmly packed brown sugar
1 egg
2 cups (300g) plain flour
¼ cup (25g) cocoa powder
1 teaspoon bicarbonate of soda
400g dark eating chocolate, chopped coarsely
candied chillies
¼ cup (55g) caster sugar
¼ cup (60ml) water
3 fresh red thai chillies, chopped finely

1 Preheat oven to 180°C/160°C fan-forced. Grease oven trays;
line with baking paper.
2 Make candied chillies.
3 Beat butter, extract, sugars and egg in small bowl with electric mixer
until light and fluffy. Transfer mixture to large bowl; stir in sifted flour,
cocoa and soda, in two batches. Stir in chilli and chocolate.
4 Roll level tablespoons of dough into balls; place about 5cm apart
on oven trays.
5 Bake cookies about 12 minutes; cool on trays.
candied chillies Stir sugar and the water in small saucepan over heat
until sugar dissolves. Add chilli, boil, 2 minutes; cool. Strain, discard syrup.

prep + cook time 30 minutes **makes** 48

choc-fudge brownie cookies

250g butter, softened
1 teaspoon vanilla extract
¾ cup (165g) caster sugar
¾ cup (165g) firmly packed brown sugar
1 egg
2 cups (300g) plain flour
¼ cup (25g) cocoa powder
1 teaspoon bicarbonate of soda
⅓ cup (45g) finely chopped roasted hazelnuts
⅔ cup (120g) coarsely chopped dark eating chocolate
⅔ cup (120g) coarsely chopped milk eating chocolate
⅔ cup (120g) coarsely chopped white eating chocolate

1 Preheat oven to 180°C/160°C fan-forced. Grease oven trays;
line with baking paper.
2 Beat butter, extract, sugars and egg in small bowl with electric mixer
until light and fluffy. Transfer mixture to large bowl; stir in sifted flour,
cocoa and soda, in two batches. Stir in nuts and chocolate.
3 Roll level tablespoons of dough into balls; place about 5cm apart
on oven trays.
4 Bake cookies about 12 minutes; cool on trays.

prep + cook time 30 minutes **makes** 48

peanut brittle cookies

125g butter, softened
¼ cup (70g) crunchy peanut butter
½ cup (100g) firmly packed brown sugar
1 egg
1½ cups (225g) plain flour
½ teaspoon bicarbonate of soda
peanut brittle
¾ cup (100g) roasted unsalted peanuts
½ cup (110g) caster sugar
2 tablespoons water

1 Preheat oven to 160°C/140°C fan-forced. Grease oven trays;
line with baking paper.
2 Make peanut brittle.
3 Beat butter, peanut butter, sugar and egg in small bowl with
electric mixer until combined. Stir in sifted dry ingredients and
crushed peanut brittle.
4 Roll heaped teaspoons of mixture into balls with floured hands.
Place about 5cm apart on oven trays; flatten slightly with hand.
5 Bake cookies about 12 minutes; cool on trays.
peanut brittle Place nuts on baking-paper-lined oven tray. Stir sugar
and the water in small frying pan over heat, without boiling, until sugar
is dissolved. Bring to the boil; boil, uncovered, without stirring, until
golden brown. Pour mixture over nuts; leave until set. Crush coarsely
in food processor.

prep + cook time 35 minutes **makes** 42

chocolate and cranberry checkerboard cookies

200g butter, softened
¾ cup (165g) caster sugar
½ teaspoon vanilla extract
1 egg
2 cups (300g) plain flour
1 tablespoon cocoa powder
1 teaspoon finely grated orange rind
¼ cup (40g) finely chopped dried cranberries
1 egg white

1 Beat butter, sugar, extract and egg in medium bowl with electric mixer until light and fluffy. Stir in sifted flour, in two batches.
2 Divide dough in half, knead sifted cocoa into one half; knead rind and cranberries into the other half. Using ruler, shape each batch of dough into 4.5cm x 4.5cm x 15cm rectangular bars. Wrap each in baking paper; refrigerate 30 minutes.
3 Cut each bar lengthways equally into three slices. Cut each slice lengthways equally into three; you will have nine 1.5cm x 1.5cm x 15cm slices from each bar of dough.
4 Brush each slice of dough with egg white, stack alternate flavours together in threes. Stick three stacks together to recreate the log; repeat with second log. Refrigerate 30 minutes.
5 Preheat oven to 180°C/160°C fan-forced. Grease oven trays; line with baking paper.
6 Using a sharp knife, cut each log crossways into 1cm slices. Place, cut-side up, onto oven trays about 3cm apart.
7 Bake cookies about 15 minutes. Stand cookies on trays 5 minutes; transfer to wire racks to cool.

prep + cook time 50 minutes (+ refrigeration) **makes** 30

honey, oat and barley horseshoes

125g butter, softened
½ cup (110g) caster sugar
1 egg
2 tablespoons golden syrup
2 tablespoons honey
½ cup (45g) rolled oats
½ cup (65g) rolled barley
2 cups (300g) plain flour
½ teaspoon bicarbonate of soda
1½ teaspoons cream of tartar
1 teaspoon ground ginger
1 teaspoon mixed spice
½ teaspoon ground clove
½ cup (45g) rolled oats, extra

1 Preheat oven to 180°C/160°C fan-forced. Grease oven trays;
line with baking paper.
2 Beat butter, sugar and egg in small bowl with electric mixer until
combined. Transfer mixture to large bowl; stir in golden syrup, honey,
oats, barley and sifted dry ingredients.
3 Knead dough on floured surface until smooth. Sprinkle surface with
extra rolled oats; roll level tablespoons of dough in oats into 12cm
sausages. Shape into horseshoes; place about 3cm apart on oven trays.
4 Bake horseshoes about 20 minutes. Cool on wire racks.

prep + cook time 40 minutes **makes** 26

snickerdoodles

250g butter, softened
1 teaspoon vanilla extract
½ cup (110g) firmly packed brown sugar
1 cup (220g) caster sugar
2 eggs
2¾ cups (410g) plain flour
1 teaspoon bicarbonate of soda
½ teaspoon ground nutmeg
1 tablespoon caster sugar, extra
2 teaspoons ground cinnamon

1 Beat butter, extract and sugars in small bowl with electric mixer until light and fluffy. Beat in eggs, one at a time. Transfer mixture to large bowl; stir in sifted flour, soda and nutmeg, in two batches. Cover; refrigerate 30 minutes.
2 Preheat oven to 180°C/160°C fan-forced. Grease oven trays; line with baking paper.
3 Combine extra caster sugar and cinnamon in small shallow bowl. Roll level tablespoons of the dough into balls; roll balls in cinnamon sugar. Place balls about 7cm apart on oven trays.
4 Bake snickerdoodles about 12 minutes; cool on trays.

prep + cook time 35 minutes (+ refrigeration) **makes** 42

macadamia anzac biscuits

125g butter, chopped
2 tablespoons golden syrup
½ teaspoon bicarbonate of soda
2 tablespoons boiling water
1 cup (90g) rolled oats
1 cup (150g) plain flour
1 cup (220g) firmly packed brown sugar
¾ cup (60g) desiccated coconut
½ cup (65g) finely chopped macadamia nuts
¼ cup (45g) finely chopped glacé ginger

1 Preheat oven to 180°C/160°C fan-forced. Grease oven trays; line with baking paper.
2 Stir butter and golden syrup in medium saucepan over low heat until smooth. Stir in soda and the water; stir in remaining ingredients.
3 Roll level tablespoons of mixture into balls. Place about 5cm apart on oven trays; flatten slightly.
4 Bake biscuits about 15 minutes; cool on trays.

prep + cook time 30 minutes **makes** 32

anzac biscuits

1 cup (90g) rolled oats
1 cup (150g) plain flour
1 cup (220g) firmly packed brown sugar
½ cup (40g) desiccated coconut
125g butter
2 tablespoons golden syrup
1 tablespoon water
½ teaspoon bicarbonate of soda

1 Preheat oven to 160°C/140°C fan-forced. Grease oven trays; line with baking paper.
2 Combine oats, sifted flour, sugar and coconut in large bowl.
3 Stir butter, syrup and the water in small saucepan over low heat until smooth; stir in soda. Stir syrup mixture into dry ingredients.
4 Roll level tablespoons of mixture into balls; place about 5cm apart on trays, flatten slightly.
5 Bake biscuits about 20 minutes; cool on trays.

prep + cook time 35 minutes **makes** 25

vanilla bean butter biscuits

125g butter, softened
½ cup (80g) icing sugar
1 vanilla bean
1 ¼ cups (185g) plain flour

1 Place butter and sifted icing sugar in small bowl. Split vanilla bean; scrape seeds into bowl. Beat mixture with electric mixer until light and fluffy; stir in sifted flour, in two batches.
2 Knead dough on floured surface until smooth. Shape dough into 25cm-rectangular log. Enclose log in plastic wrap; refrigerate about 30 minutes or until firm.
3 Preheat oven to 180°C/160°C fan-forced. Grease oven trays; line with baking paper.
4 Cut log into 1cm slices; place slices about 2cm apart on trays.
5 Bake biscuits about 12 minutes; cool on trays.

prep + cook time 30 minutes (+ refrigeration) **makes** 22

traditional shortbread

250g butter, softened
⅓ cup (75g) caster sugar
1 tablespoon water
2 cups (300g) plain flour
½ cup (100g) rice flour
2 tablespoons white sugar

1 Preheat oven to 160°C/140°C fan-forced. Grease oven trays.
2 Beat butter and caster sugar in medium bowl with electric mixer until light and fluffy. Stir in the water and sifted flours, in two batches. Knead mixture on floured surface until smooth.
3 Divide mixture in half; shape each, on separate trays, into 20cm rounds. Mark each round into 12 wedges; prick with fork. Pinch edges of rounds with fingers; sprinkle with white sugar.
4 Bake shortbread about 40 minutes. Stand shortbread on trays 5 minutes. Using sharp knife, cut into wedges along marked lines. Cool on trays.

prep + cook time 1 hour **makes** 24

pear and ginger biscuits

200g butter, softened
½ teaspoon vanilla extract
1 cup (160g) icing sugar
1 egg
¼ cup (35g) finely chopped dried pears
¼ cup (55g) coarsely chopped glacé ginger
½ cup (45g) rolled oats
1¾ cups (260g) plain flour
½ teaspoon bicarbonate of soda

1 Preheat oven to 170°C/150°C fan-forced. Grease oven trays;
line with baking paper.
2 Beat butter, extract, sifted icing sugar and egg in small bowl with
electric mixer until light and fluffy. Transfer mixture to medium bowl;
stir in pear, ginger and oats then sifted flour and soda, in two batches.
3 Roll level tablespoons of dough into balls; place on trays 3cm apart.
4 Bake biscuits about 15 minutes; cool on trays.

prep + cook time 35 minutes **makes** 30

brown sugar and pecan biscuits

200g butter, softened
½ teaspoon vanilla extract
1 cup (220g) firmly packed brown sugar
1 egg
½ cup (60g) coarsely chopped pecans
1¾ cups (260g) plain flour
½ teaspoon bicarbonate of soda

1 Preheat oven to 170°C/150°C fan-forced. Grease oven trays;
line with baking paper.
2 Beat butter, extract, sugar and egg in small bowl with electric mixer
until light and fluffy. Transfer mixture to medium bowl; stir in pecans
then sifted flour and soda, in two batches.
3 Roll level tablespoons of dough into balls; place on trays 3cm apart.
4 Bake biscuits about 15 minutes; cool on trays.

prep + cook time 1 hour **makes** 30

crunchy muesli cookies

1 cup (90g) rolled oats
1 cup (150g) plain flour
1 cup (220g) caster sugar
2 teaspoons ground cinnamon
¼ cup (35g) dried cranberries
⅓ cup (55g) finely chopped dried apricots
½ cup (70g) slivered almonds
125g butter, chopped coarsely
2 tablespoons golden syrup
½ teaspoon bicarbonate of soda
1 tablespoon boiling water

1 Preheat oven to 150°C/130°C fan-forced. Grease oven trays;
line with baking paper.
2 Combine oats, flour, sugar, cinnamon, dried fruit and nuts in large bowl.
3 Melt butter with golden syrup in small saucepan over low heat;
add combined soda and the boiling water. Stir warm butter mixture
into dry ingredients.
4 Roll level tablespoons of mixture into balls, place about 5cm apart
on oven trays; flatten slightly.
5 Bake cookies about 20 minutes; cool on trays.

prep + cook time 45 minutes **makes** 36

oat and bran biscuits

1 cup (150g) plain flour
1 cup (60g) unprocessed bran
¾ cup (60g) rolled oats
½ teaspoon bicarbonate of soda
60g butter, chopped coarsely
½ cup (110g) caster sugar
1 egg
2 tablespoons water, approximately

1 Process flour, bran, oats, soda and butter until crumbly; add sugar, egg and enough of the water to make a firm dough. Knead dough on floured surface until smooth. Cover; refrigerate 30 minutes.
2 Preheat oven to 180°C/160°C fan-forced. Grease oven trays; line with baking paper.
3 Divide dough in half; roll each half between sheets of baking paper to about 5mm thickness. Cut dough into 7cm rounds; place about 2cm apart on trays.
4 Bake biscuits about 15 minutes. Stand biscuits on trays 5 minutes; transfer to wire rack to cool.

prep + cook time 30 minutes (+ refrigeration) **makes** 30

vanilla bean thins

1 vanilla bean
30g butter, softened
¼ cup (55g) caster sugar
1 egg white, beaten lightly
¼ cup (35g) plain flour

1 Preheat oven to 200°C/180°C fan-forced. Grease oven trays;
line with baking paper.
2 Halve vanilla bean lengthways; scrape seeds into medium bowl,
discard pod. Add butter and sugar to bowl; stir until combined.
Stir in egg white and sifted flour.
3 Spoon mixture into piping bag fitted with 5mm plain tube.
Pipe 6cm-long strips (making them slightly wider at both ends)
about 5cm apart on trays.
4 Bake biscuits about 5 minutes or until edges are browned lightly;
cool on trays.

prep + cook time 25 minutes **makes** 24

golden pecan twists

⅓ cup (40g) finely chopped pecans
2 tablespoons golden syrup
125g butter, softened
¼ teaspoon vanilla extract
⅓ cup (75g) caster sugar
1 egg yolk
1 cup (150g) plain flour

1 Preheat oven to 180°C/160°C fan-forced. Grease oven trays;
line with baking paper.
2 Combine nuts and half the golden syrup in small bowl.
3 Beat butter, extract, sugar, egg yolk and remaining golden syrup in
small bowl with electric mixer until light and fluffy. Stir in sifted flour.
4 Shape rounded teaspoons of mixture into balls; roll each ball into
12cm log. Twist each log into a loop, overlapping one end over the
other. Place twists about 3cm apart on oven trays; top each twist with
½ teaspoon nut mixture.
5 Bake twists about 10 minutes; cool on trays.

prep + cook time 35 minutes **makes** 30

coffee almond biscuits

1 tablespoon instant coffee granules
3 teaspoons hot water
3 cups (360g) ground almonds
1 cup (220g) caster sugar
2 tablespoons coffee-flavoured liqueur
3 egg whites
24 coffee beans

1 Preheat oven to 180°C/160°C fan-forced. Grease oven trays;
line with baking paper.
2 Dissolve coffee in the hot water in large bowl. Add ground almonds,
sugar, liqueur and egg whites; stir until mixture forms a firm paste.
3 Roll level tablespoons of mixture into balls; place about 3cm apart
on trays, flatten slightly. Press coffee beans into tops of biscuits.
4 Bake biscuits about 15 minutes; cool on trays.

prep + cook time 30 minutes **makes** 24

chocolate lace crisps

100g dark cooking chocolate, chopped coarsely
80g butter, chopped coarsely
1 cup (220g) caster sugar
1 egg
1 cup (150g) plain flour
2 tablespoons cocoa powder
¼ teaspoon bicarbonate of soda
¼ cup (40g) icing sugar

1 Melt chocolate and butter in small saucepan over low heat.
2 Transfer chocolate mixture to medium bowl; sir in caster sugar,
egg and sifted flour, cocoa and soda. Cover; refrigerate 15 minutes or
until mixture is firm enough to handle.
3 Preheat oven to 180°C/160°C fan-forced. Grease oven trays;
line with baking paper.
4 Roll level tablespoons of mixture into balls; roll each ball in sifted icing
sugar, place about 8cm apart on trays.
5 Bake crisps about 15 minutes; cool on trays.

prep + cook time 45 minutes (+ refrigeration) **makes** 24

maple-syrup butter cookies

125g butter, softened
½ teaspoon vanilla extract
⅓ cup (80ml) maple syrup
¾ cup (110g) plain flour
¼ cup (35g) cornflour

1 Preheat oven to 180°C/160°C fan-forced. Grease oven trays;
line with baking paper.
2 Beat butter, extract and maple syrup in small bowl with electric mixer
until light and fluffy. Stir in sifted flours.
3 Spoon mixture into piping bag fitted with 1cm fluted tube. Pipe stars
about 3cm apart onto trays.
4 Bake cookies about 15 minutes; cool on trays.

prep + cook time 35 minutes **makes** 24

gingerbread christmas trees

3 cups (450g) self-raising flour
¾ cup (165g) firmly packed brown sugar
1 tablespoon ground ginger
1 teaspoon ground cinnamon
1 teaspoon ground nutmeg
½ teaspoon ground clove
185g butter, chopped coarsely
¾ cup (270g) golden syrup
1 egg
silver cachous
1 tablespoon icing sugar
royal icing
1 egg white
1½ cups (240g) pure icing sugar

1 Process flour, brown sugar, spices and butter until crumbly. Add golden syrup and egg; process until combined. Knead dough on floured surface until smooth. Cover; refrigerate 1 hour.
2 Divide dough in half; roll each half between sheets of baking paper to 5mm thickness. Refrigerate 30 minutes.
3 Preheat oven to 180°C/160°C fan-forced. Line oven trays with baking paper.
4 Cut twelve 3cm, twelve 5cm, twelve 6cm, twelve 7cm, twelve 8cm, and twelve 9cm stars from dough; transfer stars to trays. You will need to reroll the dough several times to get the correct number of stars.
5 Bake 3cm, 5cm and 6cm stars about 10 minutes and remaining stars about 12 minutes.
6 Meanwhile, make royal icing.
7 Assemble trees by joining two 9cm stars, two 8cm stars, two 7cm stars, two 6cm stars, two 5cm stars and two 3cm stars with a little royal icing between each star. Decorate trees by joining cachous to stars with a tiny dot of royal icing. Dust trees with sifted icing sugar.
royal icing Sift icing sugar through fine sieve. Beat egg white until foamy in small bowl with electric mixer; beat in icing sugar a tablespoon at a time.

prep + cook time 1 hour (+ refrigeration) **makes** 6 trees

hot cross bun cookies

125g butter, softened
²/₃ cup (150g) caster sugar
1 egg
¼ cup (40g) finely chopped mixed peel
½ cup (80g) dried currants
2 cups (300g) self-raising flour
1 teaspoon mixed spice
2 teaspoons milk
2 tablespoons ground almonds
100g marzipan
2 tablespoons apricot jam, warmed, strained

1 Preheat oven to 160°C/140°C fan-forced. Grease oven trays; line with baking paper.
2 Beat butter, sugar and egg in small bowl with electric mixer until light and fluffy. Stir in peel, currants, sifted flour and spice, and milk, in two batches.
3 Roll rounded teaspoons of mixture into balls; place about 5cm apart on oven trays.
4 Knead ground almonds into marzipan. Roll marzipan into 5mm diameter sausages; cut into 4cm lengths.
5 Brush cookies with a little milk; place marzipan crosses on cookies, press down gently.
6 Bake cookies about 15 minutes. Brush with jam; cool on trays.

prep + cook time 40 minutes **makes** 48

shortbread bars with nut crumble

250g butter, softened
½ cup (110g) caster sugar
2 cups (300g) plain flour
½ cup (100g) rice flour
nut crumble
⅓ cup (50g) plain flour
25g butter, chopped finely
2 tablespoons caster sugar
¼ cup (30g) finely chopped unsalted pistachios
¼ cup (35g) slivered almonds

1 Preheat oven to 160°C/140°C fan-forced. Grease oven trays;
line with baking paper.
2 Beat butter and sugar in medium bowl with electric mixer until light
and fluffy. Stir in sifted flours, in two batches. Knead dough on floured
surface until smooth.
3 Divide dough in half; roll each piece between sheets of baking paper
to 12cm x 24cm rectangle, place on tray. Refrigerate 30 minutes.
4 Meanwhile, make nut crumble.
5 Cut dough into 3cm x 6cm bars (you will have 32 bars); place on trays.
Press crumble mixture onto shortbread.
6 Bake shortbread about 15 minutes; cool on trays.
nut crumble Sift flour into medium bowl; rub in butter. Stir in sugar
and nuts.

prep + cook time 45 minutes (+ refrigeration) **makes** 32

spiced treacle cookies

75g butter, chopped
⅓ cup (120g) treacle
¼ cup (55g) firmly packed brown sugar
¾ cup (110g) plain flour
½ cup (75g) self-raising flour
1 teaspoon ground cinnamon
1 teaspoon mixed spice
¼ cup (30g) finely chopped walnuts
1 tablespoon brown sugar, extra

1 Preheat oven to 160°C/140°C fan-forced. Grease oven trays;
line with baking paper.
2 Stir butter, treacle and sugar in medium saucepan over low heat
until smooth; cool 5 minutes. Stir in sifted flours and spices.
3 Roll rounded teaspoons of mixture into balls, place about 5cm apart
on trays; flatten slightly. Sprinkle with combined nuts and extra sugar.
4 Bake cookies about 20 minutes; cool on trays.

prep + cook time 35 minutes **makes** 34

FILLED &
ICED BISCUITS

chocolate wheaties

90g butter
½ cup (100g) firmly packed brown sugar
1 egg, beaten lightly
¼ cup (20g) desiccated coconut
¼ cup (25g) wheatgerm
¾ cup (120g) wholemeal plain flour
½ cup (75g) white self-raising flour
150g dark eating chocolate, melted

1 Preheat oven to 180°C/160°C fan-forced. Grease oven trays.
2 Beat butter and sugar in small bowl with electric mixer until smooth; beat in egg. Stir in coconut, wheatgerm and flours.
3 Roll rounded teaspoons of mixture into balls, place about 3cm apart on trays; flatten with a fork.
4 Bake wheaties about 12 minutes or until browned. Cool on trays. Dip half of each biscuit in chocolate; leave to set on wire racks.

prep + cook time 35 minutes **makes** 35

chocolate coffee cream fancies

60g butter
1 teaspoon coffee and chicory essence
1 ½ tablespoons caster sugar
⅔ cup (100g) plain flour
60g dark eating chocolate, melted
coffee cream
1 ¼ cups (200g) icing sugar
2 teaspoons vegetable oil
¼ teaspoon coffee and chicory essence
1 tablespoon milk, approximately

1 Preheat oven to 180°C/160°C fan-forced. Grease oven trays.
2 Beat butter, essence and caster sugar in small bowl with electric mixer until light and fluffy. Stir in flour, mix to a firm dough. Cover; refrigerate 30 minutes.
3 Roll dough between sheets of baking paper until 3mm thick. Cut dough into 3.5cm rounds using a cutter; place rounds about 2cm apart on trays.
4 Bake biscuits about 8 minutes or until coloured. Stand biscuits on trays 5 minutes; transfer to wire racks to cool.
5 Meanwhile, make coffee cream.
6 Spread biscuits with coffee cream, stand on wire racks until set. Pipe or drizzle melted chocolate over biscuits.
coffee cream Sift icing sugar into small bowl; stir in oil, essence and enough milk to make spreadable.

prep + cook time 45 minutes (+ refrigeration) **makes** 40

fruit mince surprises

1 cup (150g) white self-raising flour
½ cup (80g) wholemeal plain flour
2 tablespoons wheatgerm
¼ cup (55g) caster sugar
¼ cup (50g) firmly packed brown sugar
1 teaspoon ground cinnamon
100g butter, chopped
1 egg
1 teaspoon water, approximately
½ cup (160g) fruit mince
1 tablespoon icing sugar

1 Process flours, wheatgerm, sugars, cinnamon and butter until mixture resembles breadcrumbs. Add egg and enough of the water until ingredients come together. Knead dough on floured surface until smooth. Cover; refrigerate 30 minutes.
2 Preheat oven to 180°C/160°C fan-forced. Grease oven trays.
3 Roll dough between sheets of baking paper until 4mm thick. Cut dough into rounds using 7.5cm cutter. Drop a level teaspoon of fruit mince on centre of each round, brush edges lightly with water; pinch edges together to enclose filling. Place about 3cm apart, seam-side down, on trays; flatten slightly.
4 Bake biscuits about 20 minutes or until browned. Stand biscuits on trays 5 minutes; transfer to wire racks to cool. Serve dusted with sifted icing sugar.

prep + cook time 45 minutes (+ refrigeration) **makes** 24

passionfruit creams

You need about 4 passionfruit for this recipe.

1 cup (150g) plain flour
½ cup (75g) self-raising flour
2 tablespoons cornflour
2 tablespoons custard powder
⅔ cup (110g) icing sugar
90g butter, chopped
1 egg yolk
¼ cup (60ml) passionfruit pulp
2 tablespoons icing sugar, extra
passionfruit cream
¼ cup (55g) caster sugar
1 tablespoon water
60g butter
1 tablespoon passionfruit pulp

1 Sift dry ingredients into medium bowl; rub in butter. Add egg yolk
and passionfruit pulp; mix to a firm dough. Knead dough on floured
surface until smooth. Cover; refrigerate 30 minutes.
2 Preheat oven to 180°C/160°C fan-forced. Grease oven trays.
3 Roll dough between sheets of baking paper until 3mm thick.
Cut dough into rounds using 5.5cm cutter; place rounds about
3cm apart on trays.
4 Bake biscuits about 15 minutes or until lightly browned. Stand
biscuits on trays 5 minutes; transfer to wire racks to cool.
5 Meanwhile, make passionfruit cream.
6 Spoon passionfruit cream into piping bag fitted with small fluted nozzle;
pipe cream onto each biscuit. Dust with sifted extra icing sugar.
passionfruit cream Stir sugar and the water in small saucepan over
heat until sugar is dissolved; bring to the boil. Reduce heat; simmer
2 minutes. Cool. Beat butter in small bowl with electric mixer until light
and fluffy; gradually add cold syrup, beating well between each addition.
Stir in passionfruit pulp.

prep + cook time 35 minutes (+ refrigeration) **makes** 35

vanilla melting moments

250g butter, softened
1 teaspoon vanilla extract
½ cup (80g) icing sugar
1½ cups (225g) plain flour
½ cup (75g) cornflour
1 tablespoon icing sugar, extra
butter cream
80g butter
⅔ cup (110g) icing sugar
1 teaspoon grated lemon rind
1 teaspoon lemon juice

1 Preheat oven to 180°C/160°C fan-forced. Grease oven trays; line with baking paper.
2 Beat butter, extract and sifted icing sugar in small bowl with electric mixer until light and fluffy. Stir in combined sifted flours, in two batches.
3 With floured hands, roll 2-level-teaspoons of mixture into balls. Place balls about 3cm apart on trays; flatten slightly with a floured fork.
4 Bake biscuits about 15 minutes or until a pale-straw colour. Stand biscuits on trays 5 minutes; tansfer to wire racks to cool.
5 Meanwhile, make butter cream.
6 Sandwich biscuits with a teaspoon of butter cream. Serve dusted with sifted extra icing sugar.
butter cream Beat butter, sifted icing sugar and rind in small bowl with electric mixer until pale and fluffy. Beat in juice.

prep + cook time 45 minutes **makes** 25

rhubarb custard melting moments

250g butter, softened
½ teaspoon vanilla extract
½ cup (80g) icing sugar
1 cup (125g) custard powder
1 cup (150g) plain flour
1 tablespoon icing sugar, extra
rhubarb custard
1 tablespoon custard powder
1 tablespoon caster sugar
½ cup (125ml) milk
⅓ cup stewed rhubarb (see tip)

1 Preheat oven to 160°C/140°C fan-forced. Grease oven trays;
line with baking paper.
2 Make rhubarb custard.
3 Meanwhile, beat butter, extract and sifted icing sugar in small bowl
with electric mixer until light and fluffy. Stir in sifted custard powder
and flour, in two batches.
4 With floured hands, roll rounded teaspoons of mixture into balls. Place
balls about 5cm apart on oven trays; flatten slightly with a floured fork.
5 Bake biscuits about 15 minutes. Stand biscuits on trays 5 minutes;
transfer to wire racks to cool.
6 Sandwich biscuits with a little rhubarb custard.

rhubarb custard Blend custard powder and sugar with milk in small
saucepan; stir over heat until mixture boils and thickens. Remove
from heat, stir in rhubarb. Cover surface of custard with plastic wrap;
refrigerate until cold.

prep + cook time 45 minutes **makes** 25
tip To make the stewed rhubarb, cook 1 large stem chopped rhubarb,
1 tablespoon caster sugar (or to taste) and 1 tablespoon water in small
saucepan over low heat until rhubarb is pulpy. Drain; cool.

chocolate melting moments

125g butter, softened
2 tablespoons icing sugar
¾ cup (110g) plain flour
2 tablespoons cornflour
1 tablespoon cocoa powder
¼ cup (85g) chocolate hazelnut spread

1 Preheat oven to 180°C/160°C fan-forced. Grease oven trays;
line with baking paper.
2 Beat butter and sifted icing sugar in small bowl with electric mixer
until light and fluffy. Stir in sifted dry ingredients.
3 Spoon mixture into piping bag fitted with 1cm-fluted tube. Pipe stars
about 3cm apart on trays.
4 Bake biscuits about 10 minutes; cool on trays. Sandwich biscuits with
hazelnut spread.

prep + cook time 25 minutes **makes** 20

mandarin shortbread sticks

250g butter
½ cup (80g) icing sugar
2 tablespoons rice flour
2 cups (300g) plain flour
2 tablespoons finely grated mandarin rind
¼ cup (60ml) mandarin juice
½ cup (75g) macadamias, toasted, chopped finely
60g dark eating chocolate, melted

1 Preheat oven to 180°C/160°C fan-forced. Grease oven trays;
line with baking paper.
2 Beat butter and sugar in medium bowl with electric mixer until
light and fluffy. Transfer mixture to large bowl; fold in flours, rind,
juice and nuts. Knead on floured surface until smooth.
3 Roll level tablespoons of mixture into 15cm-long sticks; place
sticks 3cm apart on trays.
4 Bake shortbread about 20 minutes or until firm. Stand shortbread
on tray 5 minutes; transfer to wire racks to cool. Pipe or drizzle melted
chocolate onto shortbread.

prep + cook time 45 minutes **makes** 35

ginger chocolate creams

125g unsalted butter, softened
1/3 cup (75g) firmly packed brown sugar
2 tablespoons golden syrup
1/2 cup (75g) self-raising flour
2/3 cup (100g) wholemeal self-raising flour
1 teaspoon ground ginger
1 tablespoon cocoa powder
ginger chocolate cream
150g milk eating chocolate, chopped coarsely
1/4 cup (60ml) cream
1/4 cup (55g) finely chopped glacé ginger

1 Beat butter and sugar in small bowl with electric mixer until light and fluffy. Beat in golden syrup. Stir in sifted dry ingredients, in two batches. Knead on floured surface until smooth.
2 Roll dough between sheets of baking paper until 5mm thick; refrigerate 30 minutes.
3 Meanwhile, make chocolate ginger cream.
4 Preheat oven to 180°C/160°C fan-forced. Grease two oven trays; line with baking paper.
5 Cut 32 x 5.5cm rounds from dough; place on trays.
6 Bake biscuits about 5 minutes; cool on trays. Sandwich biscuits with ginger chocolate cream.
ginger chocolate cream Stir chocolate and cream in small heatproof bowl over small saucepan of simmering water until smooth. Stir in ginger; refrigerate until spreadable.

prep + cook time 35 minutes **makes** 16

jammy spice drops

30g butter
⅓ cup (115g) golden syrup
1 cup (150g) plain flour
½ teaspoon bicarbonate of soda
¼ teaspoon ground ginger
¼ teaspoon ground cardamom
¼ teaspoon ground cinnamon
¼ teaspoon ground cloves
½ teaspoon cocoa powder
1 tablespoon milk
2 tablespoons finely chopped mixed peel
¼ cup (80g) raspberry jam
60g dark eating chocolate, melted

1 Melt butter in small saucepan; add syrup, bring to the boil. Remove pan from heat; stand 10 minutes. Stir in sifted dry ingredients, milk and peel. Cover; cool 2 hours.
2 Preheat oven to 180°C/160°C fan-forced. Grease two oven trays.
3 Knead dough on surface dusted with a little extra flour until dough loses stickiness.
4 Roll dough between sheets of baking paper to about 8mm thickness. Cut out rounds using 4cm-fluted round cutter. Place about 3cm apart on trays. Using end of handle of wooden spoon, gently press hollows into each round; fill with ½ teaspoon jam.
5 Bake biscuits 10 minutes; cool on trays. Spread flat-sides of biscuits with chocolate. Place biscuits, jam-side down, on foil-lined trays; set at room temperature.

prep + cook time 35 minutes (+ cooling) **makes** 24

brandy snaps with hazelnut cream

1 tablespoon golden syrup
30g butter
1½ tablespoons brown sugar
1½ tablespoons plain flour
1 teaspoon ground ginger
45 (⅓ cup) roasted hazelnuts
hazelnut cream
¾ cup (180ml) thickened cream
1 tablespoon hazelnut-flavoured liqueur

1 Preheat oven to 180°C/160°C fan-forced. Grease two oven trays.
2 Stir syrup, butter and sugar in small saucepan; stir over low heat until smooth. Remove pan from heat; stir in sifted flour and ginger.
3 Drop four level ¼-teaspoons of mixture, about 5cm apart, on oven tray (for easier handling, bake only four at a time).
4 Bake brandy snaps about 4 minutes or until golden brown. Remove from oven; cool on tray 30 seconds. With rounded knife or metal spatula, quickly lift brandy snap from tray; shape each brandy snap into a basket-shape using an upturned foil petit-four case as a guide. Repeat with remaining mixture.
5 Make hazelnut cream.
6 Just before serving, fill baskets with hazelnut cream; top each with a hazelnut.

hazelnut cream Beat ingredients in small bowl with electric mixer until firm peaks form.

prep + cook time 40 minutes **makes** 45

rum and raisin cornettes

1 egg white
⅓ cup (55g) icing sugar
½ teaspoon vanilla extract
30g butter, melted
¼ cup (30g) ground almonds
¼ cup (35g) plain flour
filling
⅓ cup (50g) finely chopped raisins
¼ cup (60ml) dark rum
1 cinnamon stick
1 cup (240g) ricotta cheese
2 tablespoons honey

1 Preheat oven to 200°C/180°C fan-forced. Grease two oven trays. Mark two 6cm-circles on each tray.
2 Beat egg white, sifted icing sugar and extract in small bowl with fork until foamy. Beat in butter, ground almonds and sifted flour.
3 Drop level teaspoons of mixture into circles, spread to fill circles.
4 Bake biscuits about 4 minutes or until edges are browned lightly (bake two cornettes at a time; they must be shaped quickly).
5 Using metal spatula, quickly lift one cornette from tray, roll into cone shape; hold gently until crisp. Repeat with remaining mixture.
6 Make filling. Spoon filling into piping bag fitted with 1cm plain tube; pipe mixture into cornettes.
filling Stir raisins, rum and cinnamon in small saucepan over low heat until warm; cool, then discard cinnamon. Combine cheese and honey in small bowl; stir in raisin mixture.

prep + cook time 45 minutes **makes** 20

sweet shortbread spirals

½ cup (110g) caster sugar
100g cold butter, chopped coarsely
1¼ cups (185g) plain flour
1 egg yolk
1 tablespoon milk
1½ cups (400g) fruit mince
¼ cup (80g) apricot jam, warmed, sieved

1 Process sugar, butter and sifted flour until crumbly. Add egg yolk and milk; process until combined. Knead dough on floured surface until smooth. Cover; refrigerate 30 minutes.
2 Meanwhile, process fruit mince until chopped finely.
3 Roll dough between two sheets of baking paper to 25cm x 30cm. Spread fruit mince evenly over rectangle, leaving 1cm border. Using paper as a guide, roll rectangle tightly from short side to enclose filling. Wrap roll in baking paper; refrigerate 30 minutes.
4 Preheat oven to 160°C/140°C fan-forced. Grease two oven trays; line with baking paper.
5 Trim edges of roll; cut roll into 1cm slices. Place slices, cut-side up, onto oven trays.
6 Bake spirals about 20 minutes. Cool on tray; brush tops with jam.

prep + cook time 50 minutes (+ refrigeration) **makes** 25

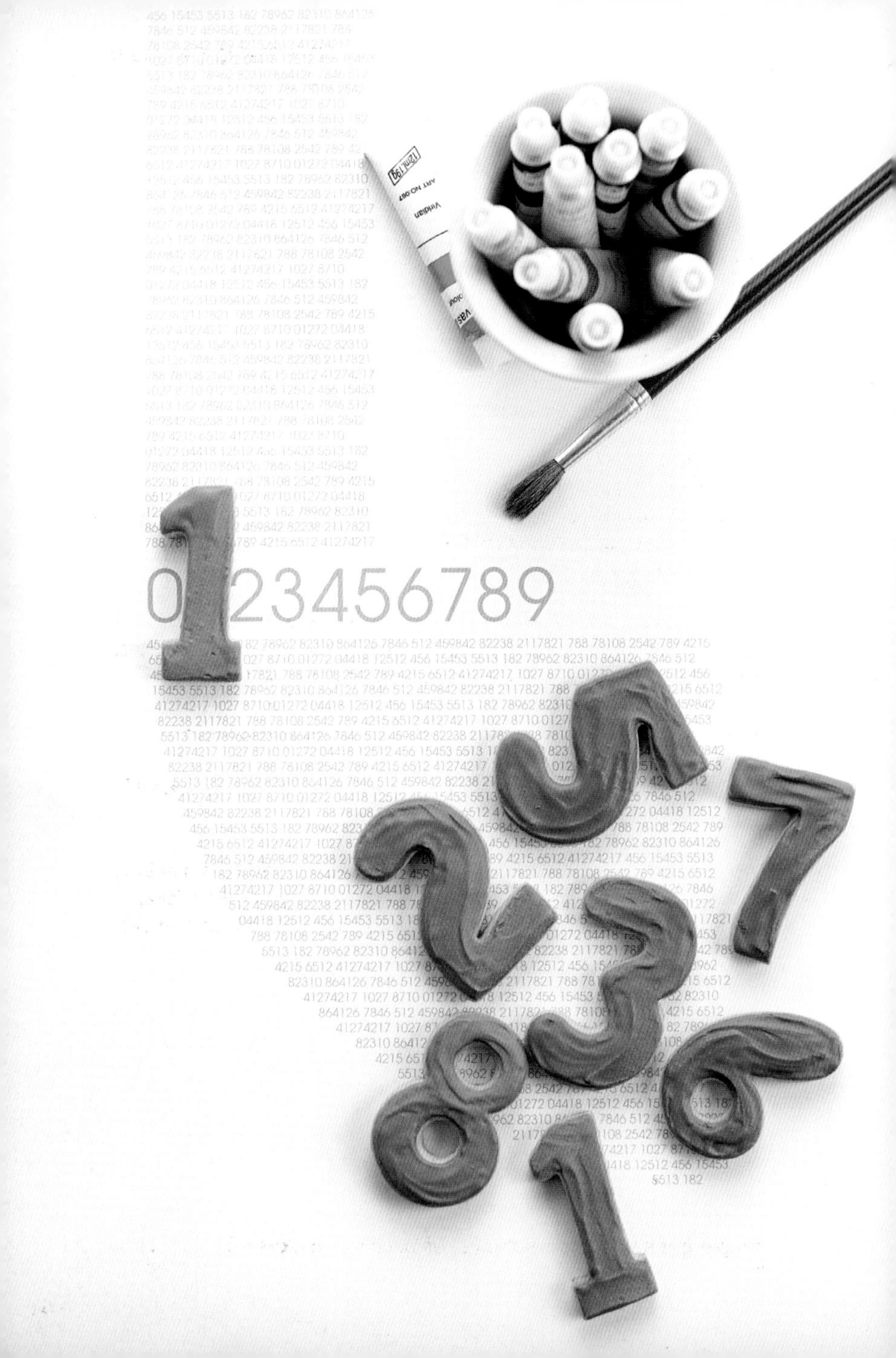
0123456789

malted milk numbers

125g butter, softened
½ cup (110g) caster sugar
1 egg
¼ cup (90g) golden syrup
¼ cup (30g) malted milk powder
2½ cups (375g) plain flour
½ teaspoon bicarbonate of soda
1½ teaspoons cream of tartar
green icing
1 egg white, beaten lightly
1½ cups (240g) icing sugar
2 teaspoons plain flour
2 teaspoons lemon juice, approximately
green food colouring

1 Beat butter, sugar and egg in small bowl with electric mixer until combined. Stir in golden syrup and sifted dry ingredients, in two batches.
2 Knead dough on floured surface until smooth; roll dough between sheets of baking paper until 5mm thick. Refrigerate 30 minutes.
3 Preheat oven to 150°C/130°C fan-forced. Grease oven trays; line with baking paper.
4 Using 6cm number cutters, cut 45 numbers from dough; place about 3cm apart on oven trays.
5 Bake biscuits about 15 minutes; cool on trays.
6 Make green icing. Spread biscuits with icing; set at room temperature.
green icing Place egg white in small bowl, stir in half the sifted icing sugar, then remaining sifted icing sugar, flour and enough juice to make a thick, spreadable icing. Tint icing green.

prep + cook time 50 minutes (+ refrigeration) **makes** 45

double chocolate freckles

125g butter, softened
¾ cup (165g) firmly packed brown sugar
1 egg
1½ cups (225g) plain flour
¼ cup (35g) self-raising flour
¼ cup (35g) cocoa powder
200g dark eating chocolate, melted
⅓ cup (85g) hundreds and thousands

1 Beat butter, sugar and egg in small bowl with electric mixer until combined. Stir in sifted dry ingredients, in two batches.
2 Knead dough on floured surface until smooth; roll dough between sheets of baking paper until 5mm thick. Refrigerate 30 minutes.
3 Preheat oven to 180°C/160°C fan-forced. Grease oven trays; line with baking paper.
4 Using 3cm, 5cm and 6.5cm round cutters, cut 14 rounds from dough using each cutter. Place 3cm rounds on one oven tray; place remainder on other oven trays.
5 Bake small cookies about 10 minutes; bake larger cookies about 12 minutes. Cool on wire racks.
6 Spread tops of cookies with chocolate; sprinkle with hundreds and thousands. Set at room temperature.

prep + cook time 45 minutes (+ refrigeration) **makes** 42

jumble bumbles

125g butter, softened
½ cup (110g) caster sugar
1 egg
¼ cup (60ml) golden syrup
2½ cups (375g) plain flour
½ teaspoon bicarbonate of soda
1½ teaspoons cream of tartar
1 teaspoon ground ginger
1 teaspoon ground mixed spice
½ teaspoon ground clove
pink icing
1 egg white, beaten lightly
1½ cups (240g) icing sugar
2 teaspoons plain flour
2 teaspoons lemon juice, approximately
pink food colouring

1 Beat butter, sugar and egg in medium bowl with electric mixer until combined. Stir in syrup and sifted dry ingredients, in two batches.
2 Knead dough on floured surface until smooth; roll dough between sheets of baking paper until 5mm thick. Refrigerate 30 minutes.
3 Preheat oven to 150°C/130°C fan-forced. Grease oven trays; ine with baking paper.
4 Using 9cm cross cutter and 7.5cm zero cutter, cut shapes from dough. Place about 3cm apart on oven trays.
5 Bake biscuit shapes about 15 minutes; cool on trays.
6 Meanwhile, make pink icing. Spread jumbles with icing; leave to set at room temperature
pink icing Place egg white in small bowl, stir in half the sifted icing sugar; add remaining sifted icing sugar, flour and enough juice to make a thick spreadable icing. Tint icing pink.

prep + cook time 45 minutes (+ refrigeration) **makes** 32

tropical florentines

⅔ cup (160ml) passionfruit pulp
¼ cup (55g) finely chopped glacé ginger
½ cup (55g) finely chopped glacé pineapple
½ cup (90g) finely chopped dried papaya
1 cup (75g) shredded coconut
1 cup (60g) coarsely crushed cornflakes
½ cup (70g) macadamias, chopped finely
¾ cup (180ml) condensed milk
1 cup (150g) white chocolate Melts

1 Preheat oven to 180°C/160°C fan-forced. Grease oven trays;
line with baking paper.
2 Strain passionfruit pulp; you need ⅓ cup (80ml) juice. Discard seeds.
3 Combine ginger, pineapple, papaya, coconut, cornflakes, nuts,
milk and 2 tablespoons of the passionfruit juice in medium bowl.
4 Drop rounded tablespoonfuls of mixture about 5cm apart onto oven
trays; press down slightly.
5 Bake florentines about 12 minutes; cool on trays.
6 Stir chocolate with remaining passionfruit juice in small heatproof
bowl over small saucepan of simmering water until smooth. Spread
chocolate over flat side of each florentine; mark with a fork. Set at
room temperature.

prep + cook time 40 minutes **makes** 25

almond and plum crescents

1½ cups (225g) plain flour
½ cup (60g) ground almonds
¼ cup (55g) caster sugar
2 teaspoons finely grated lemon rind
90g cream cheese, chopped
90g butter, chopped
2 tablespoons buttermilk
1 egg white
¼ cup (20g) flaked almonds, crushed lightly
filling
⅓ cup (60g) finely chopped seeded prunes
¼ cup (80g) plum jam
¼ cup (55g) caster sugar
½ teaspoon ground cinnamon

1 Process flour, ground almonds, sugar and rind until combined. Add cream cheese and butter, pulse until crumbly. Add buttermilk, process until ingredients come together.
2 Knead dough on floured surface until smooth. Divide dough in half. Roll each half between sheets of baking paper until large enough to be cut into 22cm rounds; cut dough using 22cm cake pan as a guide. Discard excess dough. Cover rounds; refrigerate 30 minutes.
3 Preheat oven to 180°C/160°C fan-forced. Grease oven trays; line with baking paper.
4 Make filling by combining ingredients in small bowl.
5 Cut each round into eight wedges, spread each wedge with a little filling mixture; roll from the wide end into a crescent shape. Place on oven trays, brush with egg white, sprinkle with flaked almonds.
6 Bake crescents about 25 minutes; cool on trays.

prep + cook time 50 minutes (+ refrigeration) **makes** 16

apple crumble custard creams

1 medium fresh apple (150g),
   peeled, cored, chopped coarsely
2 teaspoons water
125g butter, softened
⅓ cup (75g) firmly packed
   brown sugar
2 tablespoons apple concentrate
1 cup (150g) self-raising flour
¾ cup (110g) plain flour
¼ cup (30g) oatbran
¼ cup (20g) desiccated coconut
1 teaspoon ground cinnamon
1 tablespoon icing sugar

custard cream
1 tablespoon custard powder
1 tablespoon caster sugar
½ cup (125ml) milk
¼ teaspoon vanilla extract
125g cream cheese, softened

1 Stew apple with the water in small saucepan, covered, over medium heat until tender. Mash with a fork; cool.
2 Beat butter, sugar and concentrate in small bowl with electric mixer until combined. Transfer mixture to medium bowl; stir in sifted flours, oat bran, stewed apple, coconut and cinnamon, in two batches.
3 Knead dough on floured surface until smooth. Roll dough between sheets of baking paper until 3mm thick. Refrigerate 30 minutes.
4 Preheat oven to 180°C/160°C fan-forced. Grease oven trays; line with baking paper.
5 Using 6.5cm apple cutter, cut 40 shapes from dough. Place shapes about 3cm apart on oven trays.
6 Bake biscuits about 12 minutes. Cool on wire racks.
7 Meanwhile, make custard cream. Sandwich biscuits with custard cream. Serve dusted with sifted icing sugar.
custard cream Blend custard powder and sugar with milk and extract in small saucepan; stir over heat until mixture boils and thickens. Remove from heat, cover surface with plastic wrap; cool. Beat cream cheese in small bowl with electric mixer until smooth. Add custard; beat until combined.

prep + cook time 55 minutes (+ refrigeration) **makes** 20

decadent mocha fingers

1 teaspoon instant coffee
   granules
2 teaspoons boiling water
125g butter, softened
¾ cup (165g) firmly packed
   brown sugar
1 egg
1½ cups (225g) plain flour
¼ cup (35g) self-raising flour
¼ cup (25g) cocoa powder
75 roasted coffee beans

mocha custard
2 tablespoons custard powder
2 tablespoons caster sugar
60g dark eating chocolate,
   chopped coarsely
1 cup (250ml) milk
1 tablespoon coffee-flavoured
   liqueur

1 Blend coffee with the water. Beat butter, sugar and egg in small bowl with electric mixer until combined. Stir in coffee mixture, sifted flours and cocoa, in two batches.

2 Knead dough on floured surface until smooth; roll dough between sheets of baking paper until 4mm thick. Refrigerate 30 minutes.

3 Preheat oven to 180°C/160°C fan-forced. Grease oven trays; line with baking paper.

4 Make mocha custard.

5 Using 8.5cm square cutter, cut out 25 shapes from dough. Halve squares to make 50 rectangles; place on oven trays. Press three coffee beans on half of the rectangles.

6 Bake biscuits about 12 minutes. Cool on wire racks.

7 Spread custard over plain biscuits; top with coffee-bean topped biscuits.

mocha custard Blend custard powder, sugar and chocolate with milk in small saucepan; stir over heat until mixture boils and thickens. Remove from heat, stir in liqueur. Cover surface with plastic wrap; refrigerate until cold.

prep + cook time 50 minutes (+ refrigeration) **makes** 25

jammy flowers

125g butter, softened
½ teaspoon vanilla extract
½ cup (110g) caster sugar
1 cup (120g) ground almonds
1 egg
1 cup (150g) plain flour
1 teaspoon finely grated lemon rind
⅓ cup (110g) raspberry jam
2 tablespoons apricot jam

1 Preheat oven to 180°C/160°C fan-forced. Grease oven trays;
line with baking paper.
2 Beat butter, extract, sugar and ground almonds in small bowl with
electric mixer until light and fluffy; beat in egg. Stir in sifted flour.
3 Divide rind between both jams; mix well.
4 Roll level tablespoons of biscuit mixture into balls; place about 5cm
apart on oven trays, flatten slightly. Using end of a wooden spoon,
press a flower shape (about 1cm deep) into dough; fill each hole
with a little jam, using apricot jam for centres of flowers.
5 Bake biscuits about 15 minutes; cool on trays.

prep + cook time 40 minutes **makes** 26

mud cake sandwiches

250g butter, softened
1½ cups (330g) firmly packed
  brown sugar
2 eggs
3 cups (450g) plain flour
½ cup (75g) self-raising flour
½ cup (50g) cocoa powder
2 tablespoons cocoa powder, extra
chocolate mud cake
100g dark eating chocolate,
  chopped coarsely

150g butter, chopped
1 cup (220g) caster sugar
½ cup (125ml) water
2 tablespoons coffee liqueur
1 cup (150g) plain flour
2 tablespoons cocoa powder
2 egg yolks
chocolate ganache
⅓ cup (80ml) cream
200g dark eating chocolate,
  chopped coarsely

1 Preheat oven to 160°C/140°C fan-forced. Grease two 20cm x 30cm lamington pans; line with baking paper, extending paper 2cm above sides.
2 Make chocolate mud cake. Using 6.5cm round cutter, cut 12 rounds from each cake.
3 Meanwhile, make chocolate ganache.
4 Beat butter, sugar and eggs in small bowl with electric mixer until combined. Transfer to large bowl; stir in sifted flours and cocoa, in two batches. Knead on floured surface until smooth; divide in half, roll each half between sheets of baking paper until 5mm thick. Refrigerate 30 minutes.
5 Preheat oven to 180°C/160°C fan-forced. Grease oven trays; line with baking paper.
6 Using 6.5cm round cutter, cut 48 rounds from dough. Place about 3cm apart on oven trays. Bake about 12 minutes. Cool on wire racks.
7 Spread ganache onto underside of cookies; sandwich a mud cake round between two cookies. Using heart template, dust cookies with extra cocoa.
chocolate mud cake Stir chocolate, butter, sugar, the water and liqueur in small saucepan over low heat until smooth. Pour mixture in medium bowl; cool 10 minutes. Whisk in sifted flour and cocoa, then egg yolks. Divide mixture between pans. Bake about 25 minutes. Cool in pans.
chocolate ganache Bring cream to the boil in small saucepan; remove from heat. Add chocolate; stir until smooth. Refrigerate until spreadable.

prep + cook time 1 hour 15 minutes (+ refrigeration & cooling)
makes 24

choconut mint stacks

You need four 125g packets of After Dinner Mints for this recipe.

125g butter, softened
¾ cup (165g) firmly packed brown sugar
1 egg
1½ cups (225g) plain flour
¼ cup (35g) self-raising flour
2 tablespoons desiccated coconut
½ teaspoon coconut essence
2 tablespoons cocoa powder
40 square After Dinner Mints

1 Beat butter, sugar and egg in small bowl with electric mixer until combined. Stir in sifted flours, in two batches. Place half the mixture into another small bowl; stir in coconut and essence. Stir sifted cocoa into the other bowl.
2 Knead each portion of dough on floured surface until smooth. Roll between sheets of baking paper until 3mm thick. Refrigerate 30 minutes.
3 Preheat oven to 180°C/160°C fan-forced. Grease oven trays; line with baking paper.
4 Using 6cm square cutter, cut 30 shapes from each portion of dough. Place about 3cm apart on oven trays.
5 Bake cookies about 8 minutes. While cookies are still hot, sandwich three warm alternate-flavoured cookies with After Dinner Mints; press down gently. Cool on trays.

prep + cook time 40 minutes (+ refrigeration) **makes** 20

jaffa jelly cookies

½ cup (110g) caster sugar
2 eggs
1 cup (150g) plain flour
2 tablespoons caster sugar, extra
400g dark eating chocolate, melted
3 slices glacé orange, cut into wedges
orange jelly
1 cup (250ml) orange juice
2 tablespoons orange marmalade
85g packet orange jelly crystals

1 Make orange jelly.
2 Preheat oven to 180°C/160°C fan-forced. Grease oven trays;
line with baking paper.
3 Spread sugar evenly over base of shallow oven tray; heat in oven
until sugar feels hot to touch. Beat eggs in small bowl with electric mixer
on high speed for 1 minute; add hot sugar, beat about 10 minutes or
until mixture is thick and will hold its shape.
4 Transfer egg mixture to large bowl; fold in triple-sifted flour. Spoon
mixture into piping bag fitted with a plain 1cm tube. Pipe 4cm rounds of
mixture onto oven trays, about 3cm apart. Sprinkle each round evenly
with extra sugar.
5 Bake biscuits, one tray at a time, about 4 minutes. Cool biscuits on trays.
6 Lift jelly from pan to board. Cut out 25 rounds using a 4cm-round cutter.
7 Top each sponge with a round of jelly, place on wire rack over tray;
coat with melted chocolate. When chocolate is almost set, top with glacé
orange wedges.
orange jelly Bring juice and marmalade to the boil in small saucepan;
remove from heat. Stir in jelly crystals until dissolved; cool. Line a deep
23cm-square cake pan with baking paper, extending paper 5cm above
sides. Pour jelly into pan; refrigerate until set.

prep + cook time 1 hour 10 minutes (+ refrigeration) **makes** 24

choc-nut brandy snap wafers

60g butter
¼ cup (55g) firmly packed brown sugar
2 tablespoons golden syrup
1 teaspoon ground cinnamon
½ cup (75g) plain flour
½ cup (70g) unroasted hazelnuts, chopped coarsely
½ cup (70g) unsalted pistachios, chopped coarsely
100g dark eating chocolate, chopped finely

1 Preheat oven to 180°C/160°C fan-forced. Grease two oven trays;
line with baking paper.
2 Stir butter, sugar, golden syrup and cinnamon in small saucepan over
low heat until butter has melted. Remove from heat; stir in flour.
3 Working quickly, spread four 12cm squares of mixture about 3cm
apart onto trays. Bake 2 minutes; sprinkle with combined nuts.
Bake about 5 minutes or until brandy snaps bubble and become
golden brown.
4 Remove from oven; sprinkle with chocolate immediately. Cool on trays.
Cut into squares.

prep + cook time 35 minutes **makes** 16

glazed almond biscuits

1 cup (120g) ground almonds
1 cup (160g) icing sugar
1 egg white
glaze
2 teaspoons gelatine
2 teaspoons caster sugar
¼ cup (60ml) boiling water

1 Grease two oven trays; line with baking paper.
2 Combine biscuit ingredients in small bowl. Spoon mixture into piping bag fitted with 1cm-fluted tube; pipe shapes onto trays. Stand, uncovered, overnight to dry.
3 Preheat oven to 200°C/180°C fan-forced.
4 Bake biscuits about 5 minutes or until browned lightly.
5 Meanwhile, make glaze.
6 Cool biscuits 1 minute on trays; transfer to wire rack. Brush hot biscuits with hot glaze; cool.
glaze Stir ingredients in small jug until sugar and gelatine dissolve.

prep + cook time 40 minutes (+ standing) **makes** 40

caramel ginger crunchies

2 cups (300g) plain flour
½ teaspoon bicarbonate of soda
1 teaspoon ground cinnamon
2 teaspoons ground ginger
1 cup (220g) caster sugar
125g cold butter, chopped
1 egg
1 teaspoon golden syrup
2 tablespoons finely chopped glacé ginger
45 wrapped hard caramels

1 Preheat oven to 160°C/140°C fan-forced. Grease oven trays; line with baking paper.
2 Process sifted dry ingredients with butter until mixture is crumbly; add egg, golden syrup and ginger, process until ingredients come together. Knead on floured surface until smooth.
3 Roll rounded teaspoons of mixture into balls; flatten slightly. Place about 3cm apart on oven trays.
4 Bake biscuits 13 minutes. Remove from oven; place one caramel on top of each hot cookie. Bake about 7 minutes or until caramel begins to melt. Cool biscuits on trays.

prep + cook time 40 minutes **makes** 45

green tea and almond tiles

125g butter, softened
¼ cup (55g) caster sugar
½ teaspoon vanilla extract
1 egg
1 cup (150g) plain flour
2 tablespoons self-raising flour
¼ cup (35g) cornflour
1 tablespoon green tea leaves
   (about 4 tea bags)
½ cup (60g) ground almonds

fondant icing
300g ready-made white icing,
   chopped coarsely
1 egg white, beaten lightly
royal icing
1½ cups (240g) pure icing sugar
1 egg white
½ teaspoon vanilla extract
black food colouring

1 Beat butter, sugar, extract and egg in small bowl with electric mixer until light and fluffy. Stir in sifted flours, tea and ground almonds.
2 Knead dough on floured surface until smooth; roll dough between sheets of baking paper until 5mm thick. Refrigerate 30 minutes.
3 Preheat oven to 180°C/160°C fan-forced. Grease oven trays; line with baking paper.
4 Using 9.5cm square cutter, cut 14 squares from dough. Cut squares in half to make 28 rectangles. Place about 3cm apart on oven trays.
5 Bake biscuits about 15 minutes. Cool on wire racks.
6 Meanwhile, make fondant icing. Make royal icing.
7 Using a metal spatula dipped in hot water, spread cookies with fondant icing. Decorate with black royal icing.
fondant icing Stir ready-made icing in small heatproof bowl over small saucepan of simmering water until smooth. Stir in egg white until smooth.
royal icing Sift icing sugar through fine sieve. Beat egg white until foamy in small bowl with electric mixer; add icing sugar, a tablespoon at a time. When icing reaches firm peaks, use a wooden spoon to beat in extract and colouring; cover surface tightly with plastic wrap.

prep + cook time 1 hour 10 minutes (+ refrigeration) **makes** 28

frangipanis

185g butter, softened
1 teaspoon coconut essence
2 teaspoons finely grated lime rind
⅓ cup (75g) caster sugar
1½ cups (225g) plain flour
¼ cup (35g) rice flour
⅓ cup (30g) desiccated coconut
¼ cup (55g) finely chopped glacé pineapple
1 tablespoon purple coloured sprinkles
fondant icing
300g ready-made white icing, chopped coarsely
1 egg white, beaten lightly
pink food colouring

1 Beat butter, essence, rind and sugar in small bowl with electric mixer until smooth. Stir in sifted flours, coconut and pineapple, in two batches.
2 Knead dough on floured surface until smooth. Roll dough between sheets of baking paper until 5mm thick. Refrigerate 30 minutes.
3 Preheat oven to 160°C/140°C fan-forced. Grease round-based patty pans.
4 Using 7cm flower cutter, cut 28 shapes from dough; place in patty pans.
5 Bake biscuits about 10 minutes; cool in pans.
6 Make fondant icing. Using a metal spatula dipped in hot water, spread pink icing quickly over cookies. Sprinkle coloured sprinkles into centres of flowers.
fondant icing Stir ready-made icing in small bowl over small saucepan of simmering water until smooth. Stir in egg white until smooth. Tint with colouring.

prep + cook time 50 minutes (+ refrigeration) **makes** 28

iced marshmallow butterflies

125g butter, softened
¾ cup (165g) caster sugar
1 egg
1½ cups (225g) plain flour
¼ cup (35g) self-raising flour
½ cup (40g) desiccated coconut
⅓ cup (25g) desiccated coconut, extra
topping
160 mini pink marshmallows
160 mini white marshmallows
¼ cup (80g) strawberry jam, warmed, strained, cooled

1 Beat butter, sugar and egg in small bowl with electric mixer until light and fluffy. Stir in sifted flours and coconut, in two batches.
2 Knead dough on floured surface until smooth. Roll dough between sheets of baking paper until 5mm thick. Refrigerate 30 minutes.
3 Preheat oven to 180°C/160°C fan-forced. Grease oven trays; line with baking paper.
4 Using 11.5cm butterfly cutter, cut 16 shapes from dough. Place about 3cm apart on oven trays.
5 Bake biscuits about 12 minutes. Press marshmallows onto hot butterfly wings. Brush marshmallows with a little water; sprinkle with extra coconut. Bake about 1 minute or until marshmallows soften slightly.
6 Pipe jam down centre of each butterfly. Cool on wire racks.

prep + cook time 55 minutes (+ refrigeration) **makes** 16

choc-mallow wheels

125g butter, softened
¾ cup (165g) firmly packed brown sugar
1 egg
1½ cups (225g) plain flour
¼ cup (35g) self-raising flour
¼ cup (25g) cocoa powder
28 marshmallows
375g dark chocolate Melts
1 tablespoon vegetable oil
¼ cup (80g) raspberry jam

1 Beat butter, sugar and egg in small bowl with electric mixer until combined. Stir in sifted flours and cocoa, in two batches.
2 Knead dough on floured surface until smooth. Roll between sheets of baking paper until 3mm thick. Cover; refrigerate 30 minutes.
3 Preheat oven to 180°C/160°C fan-forced. Grease oven trays; line with baking paper.
4 Using 7cm round fluted cutter, cut 28 rounds from dough. Place about 3cm apart on trays.
5 Bake biscuits about 12 minutes. Cool on wire racks.
6 Turn half the biscuits base-side up; place on oven tray. Using scissors, cut marshmallows in half horizontally. Press four marshmallow halves, cut-side down, onto biscuit bases on tray. Bake 2 minutes.
7 Melt chocolate in medium heatproof bowl over medium saucepan of simmering water. Remove from heat; stir in oil.
8 Spread jam over bases of remaining cookies; press onto softened marshmallow. Stand 20 minutes or until marshmallow is firm. Dip wheels into chocolate; smooth away excess chocolate using metal spatula. Place on baking-paper-lined trays to set.

prep + cook time 55 minutes (+ refrigeration & standing) **makes** 28

coffee walnut creams

1²/₃ cups (250g) plain flour
125g cold butter, chopped
¼ cup (55g) caster sugar
½ teaspoon vanilla extract
1 egg, beaten lightly
18 walnut halves

walnut butter cream
185g unsalted butter, softened
¾ cup (120g) icing sugar
1 tablespoon cocoa
1 tablespoon instant
 coffee granules
1 tablespoon hot water
1¼ cups (125g) walnuts,
 chopped finely

coffee icing
1 cup (160g) icing sugar
2 teaspoons instant
 coffee granules
1 tablespoon hot water
1 teaspoon butter

1 Sift flour into medium bowl, rub in butter. Stir in sugar, extract and egg.
2 Knead dough on floured surface until smooth. Divide in half;
roll each half between sheets of baking paper until 3mm thick.
Refrigerate 30 minutes.
3 Preheat oven to 180°C/160°C fan-forced. Grease oven trays;
line with baking paper.
4 Using 5.5cm round cutter, cut out 36 rounds. Place on oven trays;
bake about 12 minutes. Cool on wire racks.
5 Meanwhile, make walnut butter cream.
6 Sandwich cookies with butter cream; refrigerate 30 minutes.
7 Meanwhile, make coffee icing.
8 Spread cookies with icing and top with walnut halves.

walnut butter cream Beat butter and sifted icing sugar in small bowl
with electric mixer until light and fluffy. Beat in combined cocoa, coffee
and the water. Stir in nuts.

coffee icing Sift icing sugar into small heatproof bowl; stir in combined
coffee and the water. Add butter; stir over small saucepan of simmering
water until icing is spreadable.

prep + cook time 55 minutes (+ refrigeration) **makes** 18

chocolate lady's kisses

80g butter, softened
½ teaspoon vanilla extract
¼ cup (55g) caster sugar
1 egg
½ cup (50g) ground hazelnuts
¾ cup (110g) plain flour
¼ cup (25g) cocoa powder
1 tablespoon cocoa powder, extra
choc-hazelnut cream
100g dark eating chocolate, melted
50g butter
⅓ cup (110g) chocolate hazelnut spread

1 Beat butter, extract, sugar and egg in small bowl with electric mixer until combined. Stir in ground hazelnuts, then sifted flour and cocoa.
2 Roll dough between sheets of baking paper until 3mm thick. Refrigerate 1 hour.
3 Make choc-hazelnut cream.
4 Preheat oven to 180°C/160°C fan-forced. Grease oven trays; line with baking paper.
5 Using 4cm fluted cutter, cut 52 rounds from dough. Place on trays.
6 Bake biscuits about 8 minutes. Stand biscuits on trays 5 minutes; transfer to wire racks to cool.
7 Spoon choc-hazelnut cream into piping bag fitted with large fluted tube. Pipe cream onto one biscuit; top with another biscuit. Repeat with remaining biscuits and cream. Dust with extra sifted cocoa.
choc-hazelnut cream Beat cooled chocolate, butter and spread in small bowl with electric mixer until thick and glossy.

prep + cook time 50 minutes (+ refrigeration) **makes** 26

praline custard creams

1 cup (150g) plain flour
1¼ cups (90g) ground almonds
90g cold butter, chopped
1 egg yolk
1 teaspoon vanilla extract
2 tablespoons icing sugar
almond praline
½ cup (40g) flaked almonds
½ cup (110g) caster sugar
2 tablespoons water

custard filling
⅓ cup (75g) caster sugar
¼ cup (35g) plain flour
2 egg yolks
1 cup (250ml) milk
125g butter, softened
1 teaspoon vanilla extract
½ cup (80g) icing sugar

1 Make almond praline and custard filling.
2 Preheat oven to 160°C/140°C fan-forced. Grease oven trays;
line with baking paper.
3 Process flour, ground almonds and butter until crumbly. Add egg yolk
and extract; pulse until combined.
4 Knead dough on floured surface until smooth. Roll dough between
sheets of baking paper until 3mm thick. Using 3.5cm round cutter,
cut 72 rounds from dough. Place about 2cm apart on oven trays.
5 Bake biscuits about 12 minutes; cool on trays.
6 Sandwich cookies with custard filling. Spread a little more custard
filling around side of cookies. Roll cookies in praline then dust with
sifted icing sugar.

almond praline Place nuts on baking-paper-lined oven tray. Stir sugar
and the water in small fying pan over heat, without boiling, until sugar is
dissolved. Bring to the boil; boil, uncovered, without stirring, until golden
brown. Pour toffee over nuts; set at room temperature. Crush praline
finely in food processor.

custard filling Combine sugar and flour in small saucepan; gradually stir
in combined yolks and milk until smooth. Cook, stirring, until mixture boils
and thickens. Simmer, stirring, over low heat, 1 minute; remove from heat.
Cover surface of custard with plastic wrap; refrigerate until cold. Beat
butter and extract until mixture is as white as possible. Beat in sifted icing
sugar. Beat in cooled custard, in four batches, until smooth.

prep + cook time 1 hour 10 minutes (+ refrigeration & cooling)
makes 26

cinnamon brandy snaps with orange cream

60g butter
⅓ cup (75g) firmly packed brown sugar
2 tablespoons golden syrup
⅓ cup (50g) plain flour
2 teaspoons ground cinnamon
1 teaspoon ground ginger
300ml thickened cream
1 tablespoon icing sugar
2 teaspoons orange-flavoured liqueur

1 Preheat oven to 180°C/160°C fan-forced. Grease oven trays;
line with baking paper.
2 Stir butter, brown sugar and syrup in small saucepan over low heat
until smooth. Remove from heat; stir in sifted flour and spices.
3 Drop rounded teaspoons of mixture about 5cm apart on trays.
4 Bake snaps about 7 minutes or until they bubble. Slide spatula under
each snap to loosen; working quickly, wrap one snap around handle
of a wooden spoon. Remove handle; place snap on wire rack to cool.
Repeat with remaining snaps.
5 Beat cream, sifted icing sugar and liqueur in small bowl with electric
mixer until firm peaks form. Just before serving, fill snaps with cream.

prep + cook time 35 minutes **makes** 18
tip If snaps become cold on the tray, they will harden and be difficult to
roll. If this happens, return snaps to oven for about 1 minute to soften.

orange hazelnut butter yo-yos

250g unsalted butter, softened
1 teaspoon vanilla extract
½ cup (80g) icing sugar
1½ cups (225g) plain flour
½ cup (75g) cornflour
orange hazelnut butter
80g unsalted butter, softened
2 teaspoons finely grated orange rind
⅔ cup (110g) icing sugar
1 tablespoon ground hazelnuts

1 Preheat oven to 160°C/140°C fan-forced. Grease oven trays;
line with baking paper.
2 Beat butter, extract and sifted icing sugar in small bowl with electric
mixer until light and fluffy; stir in sifted dry ingredients, in two batches.
3 Roll rounded teaspoons of mixture into balls; place about 3cm apart
on trays. Using fork dusted with flour, press tines gently onto each
biscuit to flatten slightly.
4 Bake biscuits about 15 minutes; cool on trays.
5 Meanwhile, make orange hazelnut butter.
6 Sandwich biscuits with orange hazelnut butter; dust with a little sifted
icing sugar, if you like.
orange hazelnut butter Beat butter, rind and sifted icing sugar in small
bowl with electric mixer until light and fluffy. Stir in ground hazelnuts.

prep + cook time 30 minutes **makes** 20

hazelnut pinwheels

1¼ cups (185g) plain flour
100g butter, chopped
½ cup (110g) caster sugar
1 egg yolk
1 tablespoon milk, approximately
⅓ cup (110g) chocolate hazelnut spread
2 tablespoons ground hazelnuts

1 Process flour, butter and sugar until crumbly. Add egg yolk; process with enough milk until mixture forms a ball. Knead dough on floured surface until smooth. Cover; refrigerate 1 hour.
2 Roll dough between sheets of baking paper to form 20cm x 30cm rectangle; remove top sheet of paper. Spread dough evenly with spread; sprinkle with ground hazelnuts. Using paper as a guide, roll dough tightly from long side to enclose filling. Enclose roll in plastic wrap; refrigerate 30 minutes.
3 Preheat oven to 180°C/160°C fan-forced. Grease oven trays; line with baking paper.
4 Remove plastic from dough; cut roll into 1cm slices. Place slices on trays 2cm apart.
5 Bake pinwheels about 20 minutes. Stand pinwheels on trays 5 minutes; transfer to wire rack to cool.

prep + cook time 40 minutes (+ refrigeration) **makes** 30

chocolate ginger easter eggs

125g butter, softened
¾ cup (165g) firmly packed brown sugar
1 egg
2 tablespoons finely chopped glacé ginger
1½ cups (225g) plain flour
¼ cup (35g) self-raising flour
¼ cup (25g) cocoa powder
chocolate fondant icing
300g chocolate ready-made icing, chopped coarsely
1 egg white, beaten lightly
royal icing
1½ cups (240g) pure icing sugar
1 egg white
pink, green, blue and yellow food colouring

1 Beat butter, sugar and egg in small bowl with electric mixer until combined. Stir in ginger then sifted flours and cocoa, in two batches.
2 Knead dough on floured surface until smooth. Roll dough between sheets of baking paper until 5mm thick; refrigerate 30 minutes.
3 Preheat oven to 180°C/160°C fan-forced. Grease oven trays; line with baking paper.
4 Using 2.5cm, 4cm, 5.5cm and 7cm oval cutters, cut 13 shapes from dough with each cutter. Place about 3cm apart on oven trays.
5 Bake small cookies about 10 minutes; bake larger cookies about 12 minutes. Cool on wire racks.
6 Make chocolate fondant icing. Use a metal spatula, dipped in hot water, to spread icing quickly over cookies. Set at room temperature.
7 Make royal icing. Divide icing among four small bowls; tint each bowl with food colouring. Pipe patterns with coloured icing on cookies.
chocolate fondant icing Stir ready-made icing in small heatproof bowl over small saucepan of simmering water until smooth. Stir in egg white. Stand at room temperature about 10 minutes or until thickened slightly.
royal icing Sift icing sugar through fine sieve. Beat egg white until foamy in small bowl with electric mixer; beat in icing sugar, a tablespoon at a time. Cover surface tightly with plastic wrap.

prep + cook time 1 hour 15 minutes (+ refrigeration) **makes** 52

stained glass christmas trees

1 vanilla bean
250g butter, softened
¾ cup (165g) caster sugar
1 egg
1 tablespoon water
2¼ cups (335g) plain flour
90g individually wrapped sugar-free fruit drops,
   assorted colours

1 Split vanilla bean in half lengthways; scrape seeds into medium bowl with butter, sugar, egg and the water. Beat with an electric mixer until combined. Stir in sifted flour, in two batches.
2 Knead dough on floured surface until smooth. Cover; refrigerate 30 minutes.
3 Preheat oven to 180°C/160°C fan-forced. Line two oven trays with baking paper.
4 Using a rolling pin, gently tap wrapped lollies to crush them slightly. Unwrap lollies, separate by colour into small bowls.
5 Roll dough between sheets of baking paper to 4mm thickness. Cut shapes from dough using 8cm long Christmas tree cutter; place cookies on oven trays. Use a 4cm long Christmas tree or 1.5cm star cutter to cut out the centre of each tree to make windows. Using a skewer, make a small hole in the top of each tree for threading through ribbon.
6 Bake biscuits 7 minutes. Remove trays from oven; fill each window in trees with a few of the same-coloured lollies. Bake a further 5 minutes or until browned lightly. Cool on trays.

prep + cook time 55 minutes (+ refrigeration) **makes** 32

lemon glazed christmas wreaths

3 cups (450g) self-raising flour
125g butter
¼ cup (60ml) milk
⅔ cup (110g) caster sugar
1 teaspoon vanilla extract
2 eggs
silver edible glitter, to decorate
lemon icing
3 cups (480g) icing sugar
2 tablespoons lemon juice, approximately

1 Preheat oven to 180°C/160°C fan-forced. Grease oven trays;
line with baking paper.
2 Sift flour into medium bowl, rub in butter. Stir milk and sugar in
small saucepan over low heat until sugar is dissolved, add extract; cool
5 minutes. Stir combined warm milk mixture and egg into flour mixture.
3 Knead dough on floured surface until smooth. Roll rounded teaspoons
of dough into 13cm sausages. Twist two sausages together, form into
circles; press edges together. Place about 3cm apart on oven trays.
4 Bake biscuits about 15 minutes. Cool on wire racks.
5 Meanwhile, make lemon icing. Drizzle wreaths with icing; set at room
temperature. Sprinkle with edible glitter.
lemon icing Sift icing sugar into small heatproof bowl; stir in enough
juice to make a firm paste. Stir over small saucepan of simmering water
until pourable.

prep + cook time 45 minutes **makes** 30

angel gift tags

125g butter, softened
¾ cup (165g) caster sugar
1 egg
1¾ cups (255g) plain flour
⅓ cup (50g) self-raising flour
2 tablespoons coarse white sugar crystals
red ribbon
lemon royal icing
2 cups (320g) pure icing sugar
1 egg white
2 teaspoons lemon juice

1 Beat butter, caster sugar and egg in small bowl with electric mixer until light and fluffy. Stir in sifted flours, in two batches. Knead dough on floured surface until smooth. Cover; refrigerate 30 minutes.
2 Preheat oven to 180°C/160°C fan-forced. Line two oven trays with baking paper.
3 Roll dough between sheets of baking paper to 5mm thickness. Cut twenty 8cm x 11cm angel shapes from dough; cut two 1.5cm moon shapes from each shoulder of angel shapes for threading ribbon. Place on trays.
4 Bake biscuits about 12 minutes; cool on trays.
5 Meanwhile, make lemon royal icing.
6 Spread angels with icing; sprinkle with sugar crystals. Set icing at room temperature; thread ribbon through holes.
lemon royal icing Sift icing sugar through fine sieve. Beat egg white until foamy in small bowl with electric mixer; beat in icing sugar a tablespoon at a time. Stir in juice.

prep + cook time 50 minutes (+ refrigeration) **makes** 20

christmas pudding cookies

1⅔ cups (250g) plain flour
⅓ cup (40g) ground almonds
⅓ cup (75g) caster sugar
1 teaspoon mixed spice
1 teaspoon vanilla extract
125g cold butter, chopped
2 tablespoons water
700g rich dark fruit cake
⅓ cup (80ml) brandy
1 egg white
400g dark eating chocolate, melted
½ cup (75g) white chocolate Melts, melted
30 red glacé cherries

1 Process flour, ground almonds, sugar, spice, extract and butter until crumbly. Add the water, process until ingredients come together.
2 Knead dough on floured surface until smooth; roll dough between sheets of baking paper until 5mm thick. Refrigerate 30 minutes.
3 Preheat oven to 180°C/160°C fan-forced. Grease oven trays; line with baking paper.
4 Using 5.5cm round cutter, cut 30 rounds from dough. Place about 3cm apart on oven trays.
5 Bake biscuits about 10 minutes.
6 Meanwhile, crumble fruit cake into medium bowl; add brandy. Press mixture firmly into round metal tablespoon measures. Brush partially baked cookies with egg white, top with cake domes; bake further 5 minutes. Cool on wire racks.
7 Place wire racks over oven tray, coat cookies with dark chocolate; set at room temperature. Spoon white chocolate over cookies; top with cherries.

prep + cook time 50 minutes (+ refrigeration) **makes** 30

caramel tarts

18 (220g) butternut snap biscuits
395g can sweetened condensed milk
60g butter, chopped coarsely
⅓ cup (75g) firmly packed brown sugar
1 tablespoon lemon juice

1 Preheat oven to 160°C/140°C fan-forced. Grease two 12-hole
(1½-tablespoon/30ml) shallow round-based patty pans.
2 Place one biscuit over top of 18 pan holes; bake about 4 minutes
or until biscuits soften. Using the back of a teaspoon, gently press
softened biscuits into pan holes; cool.
3 Stir condensed milk, butter and sugar in small heavy-based
saucepan over heat until smooth. Bring to the boil; boil, stirring,
about 10 minutes or until mixture is thick and dark caramel in colour.
Remove from heat; stir in juice.
4 Spoon caramel mixture into biscuit cases; refrigerate 30 minutes or
until set.

prep + cook time 35 minutes (+ refrigeration) **makes** 18

MERINGUES
& MACAROONS

meringue kisses with passionfruit cream

cornflour
1 egg white
½ teaspoon white vinegar
⅓ cup (75g) caster sugar
1 teaspoon icing sugar
¼ cup (60ml) thickened cream
1 tablespoon passionfruit pulp
1 tablespoon icing sugar, extra

1 Preheat oven to 120°C/100°C fan-forced. Grease oven trays;
dust with a little cornflour, shaking off excess.
2 Beat egg white, vinegar and caster sugar in small bowl with electric
mixer about 10 minutes or until sugar dissolves; fold in sifted icing sugar.
3 Place meringue mixture in piping bag fitted with a small plain nozzle;
pipe 1.5cm rounds 3cm apart on trays.
4 Bake meringues about 30 minutes or until crisp and dry. Cool on trays.
5 Beat cream, passionfruit and 2 teaspoons of the extra sifted icing
sugar in small bowl with electric mixer until stiff peaks form.
6 Sandwich meringues together with passionfruit cream; dust with
remaining extra sifted icing sugar.

prep + cook time 1 hour **makes** 35

orange almond macaroons

3 egg whites
¼ cup (55g) caster sugar
orange food colouring
1¼ cups (200g) icing sugar
1 cup (120g) ground almonds
1 teaspoon finely grated orange rind
2 tablespoons flaked almonds
⅓ cup (115g) orange marmalade

1 Grease oven trays; line with baking paper.
2 Beat egg whites in small bowl with electric mixer until soft peaks form. Add caster sugar and a few drops of colouring, beat until sugar dissolves; transfer to large bowl. Fold in sifted icing sugar, ground almonds and rind, in two batches.
3 Spoon mixture into piping bag fitted with 2cm plain tube. Pipe 4cm rounds about 2cm apart onto trays. Tap trays on bench so macaroons spread slightly. Sprinkle macaroons with flaked almonds; stand 30 minutes.
4 Meanwhile, preheat oven to 150°C/130°C fan-forced.
5 Bake macaroons about 20 minutes; cool on trays.
6 Sandwich macaroons with marmalade.

prep + cook time 40 minutes (+ standing & cooling) **makes** 16
tips Unfilled macaroons will keep in an airtight container for about a week. Fill macaroons just before serving. If the marmalade is too chunky or thick to spread, warm it, strain it, and leave it cool before using.

coffee meringue kisses

¾ cup (165g) caster sugar
1 teaspoon instant coffee granules
¼ cup (60ml) water
1 egg white
1 teaspoon malt vinegar
2 teaspoons cornflour
coffee butter cream
1 teaspoon instant coffee granules
2 teaspoons hot water
2 teaspoons coffee-flavoured liqueur
60g unsalted butter, softened
⅔ cup (110g) icing sugar

1 Preheat oven to 120°C/100°C fan-forced. Grease four oven trays; line with baking paper.
2 Stir sugar, coffee and the water in small saucepan over heat until sugar is dissolved. Bring to the boil; remove pan from heat.
3 Beat egg white, vinegar and cornflour in small heatproof bowl with electric mixer until foamy. With motor operating, pour in hot syrup in a thin, steady stream; beat about 10 minutes or until mixture is thick.
4 Spoon meringue into piping bag fitted with 5mm-fluted tube; pipe meringues, about 2.5cm in diameter, about 3cm apart, on trays.
5 Bake meringues about 30 minutes or until dry to touch. Cool on trays.
6 Meanwhile, make coffee butter cream.
7 Sandwich meringues with butter cream just before serving.
coffee butter cream Dissolve coffee in the water; add liqueur. Beat butter and sifted icing sugar until light and fluffy; beat in coffee mixture.

prep + cook time 1 hour **makes** 45

strawberry meringues

1 egg white
¼ cup (55g) caster sugar
2 teaspoons caster sugar, extra
1 tablespoon raspberry jam, warmed, sieved
2 teaspoons orange-flavoured liqueur
75g small strawberries, quartered

1 Preheat oven to 120°C/100°C fan-forced. Place petit four cases on oven tray.
2 Beat egg white and 2 tablespoons of the sugar in small bowl with electric mixer until sugar is dissolved; fold in remaining 1 tablespoon sugar.
3 Drop rounded teaspoons of mixture into cases. Sprinkle meringues with extra sugar.
4 Bake meringues about 25 minutes or until they are dry to touch. Cool meringues in oven with door ajar.
5 Meanwhile, stir jam and liqueur in small saucepan over low heat until warm.
6 Gently press berries into top of each meringue; brush with warm jam mixture. Serve immediately.

prep + cook time 45 minutes **makes** 20

chocolate almond macaroons

3 egg whites
¼ cup (55g) caster sugar
1 cup (160g) icing sugar
¼ cup (25g) cocoa powder
1 cup (120g) ground almonds
2 teaspoons cocoa powder, extra
¼ cup (60ml) cream
150g dark eating chocolate, chopped finely

1 Grease oven trays; line with baking paper.
2 Beat egg whites in small bowl with electric mixer until soft peaks form. Add caster sugar, beat until sugar dissolves; transfer to large bowl. Fold in sifted icing sugar and cocoa and ground almonds, in two batches.
3 Spoon mixture into piping bag fitted with 2cm plain tube. Pipe 4cm rounds about 2cm apart onto trays. Tap trays on bench so macaroons spread slightly. Dust macaroons with extra sifted cocoa; stand 30 minutes.
4 Meanwhile, preheat oven to 150°C/130°C fan-forced.
5 Bake macaroons about 20 minutes; cool on trays.
6 Bring cream to the boil in small saucepan, remove from heat; add chocolate, stir until smooth. Refrigerate about 20 minutes or until spreadable.
7 Sandwich macaroons with chocolate filling.

prep + cook time 40 minutes (+ standing & refrigeration) **makes** 16
tip Unfilled macaroons will keep in an airtight container for about a week. Fill macaroons just before serving.

nutty meringue sticks

3 egg whites
¾ cup (165g) caster sugar
1¼ cups (120g) ground hazelnuts
1½ cups (185g) ground almonds
¼ cup (35g) plain flour
100g dark eating chocolate, melted

1 Preheat oven to 160°C/140°C fan-forced. Grease oven trays;
line with baking paper.
2 Beat egg whites in small bowl with electric mixer until foamy. Gradually
beat in sugar, one tablespoon at a time, until dissolved between additions.
Transfer mixture to large bowl; fold in ground nuts and sifted flour.
3 Spoon meringue mixture into large piping bag fitted with 1.5cm plain
tube. Pipe 8cm sticks onto trays.
4 Bake meringues about 15 minutes. Cool on trays 5 minutes; transfer
to wire racks to cool.
5 Drizzle sticks with melted chocolate, place on baking-paper-lined
trays to set.

prep + cook time 45 minutes **makes** 35

coffee hazelnut meringues

2 egg whites
½ cup (110g) caster sugar
2 teaspoons instant coffee granules
½ teaspoon hot water
3 teaspoons coffee-flavoured liqueur
¼ cup (35g) roasted hazelnuts

1 Preheat oven to 120°C/100°C fan-forced. Grease oven trays;
line with baking paper.
2 Beat egg whites in small bowl with electric mixer until soft peaks form.
Gradually add sugar, beating until dissolved between additions.
3 Meanwhile, dissolve coffee in the water in small jug; stir in liqueur.
Fold coffee mixture into meringue mixture.
4 Spoon mixture into piping bag fitted with 5mm fluted tube. Pipe
meringues onto trays 2cm apart; top each meringue with a nut.
5 Bake meringues about 45 minutes. Cool in oven with door ajar.

prep + cook time 55 minutes (+ cooling) **makes** 30

almond macaroons

2 egg whites
½ cup (110g) caster sugar
1¼ cups (150g) ground almonds
½ teaspoon almond essence
2 tablespoons plain flour
¼ cup (40g) blanched almonds

1 Preheat oven to 150°C/130°C fan-forced. Grease oven trays.
2 Beat egg whites in small bowl with electric mixer until soft peaks form; gradually add sugar, beating until dissolved between additions. Gently fold in ground almonds, essence and sifted flour, in two batches.
3 Drop level tablespoons of mixture about 5cm apart on trays; press one nut onto each macaroon.
4 Bake macaroons about 20 minutes or until firm and dry; cool on trays.

prep + cook time 35 minutes **makes** 22

pistachio, white chocolate and honey french macaroons

⅓ cup (45g) unsalted, roasted, shelled pistachios
3 egg whites
¼ cup (55g) caster sugar
green food colouring
1¼ cups (200g) icing sugar
¾ cup (90g) ground almonds
honeyed white chocolate ganache
¼ cup (60ml) cream
155g white eating chocolate, chopped coarsely
2 teaspoons honey

1 Preheat oven to 150°C/130°C fan-forced. Grease oven trays;
line with baking paper.
2 Process nuts until finely ground.
3 Beat egg whites in small bowl with electric mixer until soft peaks form.
Add caster sugar and few drops colouring, beat until sugar dissolves;
transfer mixture to large bowl. Fold in ¼ cup of the ground pistachios,
sifted icing sugar and ground almonds, in two batches.
4 Spoon mixture into piping bag fitted with 1cm plain tube. Pipe 4cm
rounds about 2.5cm apart onto trays. Tap trays on bench so macaroons
spread slightly. Sprinkle macaroons with remaining ground pistachios;
stand 30 minutes.
5 Bake macaroons about 20 minutes. Cool on trays.
6 Meanwhile, make honeyed white chocolate ganache.
7 Sandwich macaroons with ganache.
honeyed white chocolate ganache Bring cream to the boil in small
saucepan. Remove from heat; pour over chocolate and honey in small
bowl, stir until smooth. Stand at room temperature until spreadable.

prep + cook time 45 minutes (+ standing) **makes** 16

lemon coconut macaroons

3 egg whites
2 tablespoons caster sugar
1¼ cups (200g) icing sugar
½ cup (60g) ground almonds
½ cup (40g) desiccated coconut
1 tablespoon icing sugar, extra
lemon cream
300ml thickened cream
1 tablespoon icing sugar
1 teaspoon finely grated lemon rind

1 Preheat oven to 150°C/130°C fan-forced. Grease four oven trays;
line with baking paper.
2 Beat egg whites in small bowl with electric mixer until soft peaks form;
add caster sugar, beating until dissolved between additions. Transfer
mixture to large bowl. Fold in sifted icing sugar, ground almonds and
coconut, in two batches.
3 Spoon mixture into large piping bag fitted with 1.5cm plain tube. Pipe
4cm rounds, about 2cm apart, onto trays. Tap trays on bench to help
macaroons spread slightly. Dust macaroons with extra sifted icing sugar;
stand 15 minutes.
4 Meanwhile, make lemon cream.
5 Bake macaroons 20 minutes. Stand macaroons on trays 5 minutes;
transfer to wire rack to cool.
6 Sandwich macaroons with lemon cream just before serving.
lemon cream Beat ingredients in small bowl with electric mixer until
firm peaks form.

prep + cook time 1 hour (+ standing) **makes** 24

fruity popcorn macaroons

3 egg whites
¾ cup (165g) caster sugar
½ cup (40g) desiccated coconut
2 tablespoons plain flour
2 cups (20g) air-popped popcorn
½ cup (80g) finely chopped dried apricots

1 Preheat oven to 150°C/130°C fan-forced. Grease oven trays;
line with baking paper.
2 Beat egg whites in small bowl with electric mixer until soft peaks
form; gradually add sugar, beating until dissolved between additions.
Transfer mixture to large bowl; fold in coconut and sifted flour, then
popcorn and apricots.
3 Drop heaped tablespoons of mixture about 5cm apart onto trays.
4 Bake macaroons about 20 minutes; cool on trays.

prep + cook time 35 minutes **makes** 24
tip You need unflavoured, unsalted popcorn for this recipe. If you can't
find it, you need to pop 2 tablespoons of popping corn to get 2 cups.
Put the corn into a large saucepan with a tight-fitting lid. Put the pan over
a medium heat and wait until you hear the popping. Carefully shake the
pan over the heat — wait until the popping stops completely then remove
the pan from the heat. Wait a minute or two before removing the lid.

jewelled macaroons

1 egg white
¼ cup (55g) caster sugar
¾ cup (60g) shredded coconut
2 tablespoons finely chopped glacé apricot
2 tablespoons finely chopped glacé pineapple
2 tablespoons finely chopped glacé red cherries
2 tablespoons finely chopped glacé green cherries
2 tablespoons finely chopped unsalted, roasted pistachios

1 Preheat oven to 150°C/130°C fan-forced. Line two 12-hole (1-tablespoon/20ml) mini muffin pans with paper cases.
2 Beat egg white in small bowl with electric mixer until soft peaks form; gradually add sugar, beating until dissolved between additions. Fold coconut and half the combined fruit and nuts into egg white mixture.
3 Spoon mixture into paper cases. Sprinkle with remaining fruit and nut mixture.
4 Bake macaroons about 20 minutes; cool in pans.

prep + cook time 45 minutes (+ cooling) **makes** 24
tips You need about 50g of each glacé fruit. Cover macaroons with foil halfway through baking time if fruit on top starts to brown.

little apricot macaroons

¼ cup (40g) finely chopped dried apricots
1 teaspoon orange-flavoured liqueur
1 egg white
¼ cup (55g) caster sugar
1 cup (75g) desiccated coconut
1 tablespoon finely chopped white eating chocolate

1 Preheat oven to 150°C/130°C fan-forced. Line two 12-hole
(1-tablespoon/20ml) mini muffin pans with paper cases.
2 Combine apricots and liqueur in small bowl.
3 Beat egg whites in another small bowl with electric mixer until
soft peaks form; gradually add sugar, beating until dissolved between
additions. Fold in apricot mixture, coconut and chocolate.
4 Place 1 heaped teaspoon in each paper case.
5 Bake macaroons about 20 minutes; cool in pans.

prep + cook time 45 minutes **makes** 24

choc-cherry macaroon hearts

100g butter, softened
½ cup (150g) caster sugar
1 egg
2 cups (300g) plain flour
1 tablespoon cocoa powder
100g dark eating chocolate, melted
macaroon filling
1 egg white
¼ cup (55g) caster sugar
½ teaspoon vanilla extract
¾ cup (60g) desiccated coconut
1 teaspoon plain flour
2 tablespoons finely chopped red glacé cherries

1 Make macaroon filling.
2 Beat butter, sugar and egg in small bowl with electric mixer until light and fluffy; stir in sifted dry ingredients, in two batches. Stir in chocolate.
3 Knead dough on floured surface until smooth. Roll dough between sheets of baking paper until 7mm thick.
4 Preheat oven to 180°C/160°C fan-forced. Grease oven trays; line with baking paper.
5 Using 8cm heart-shaped cutter, cut hearts from dough. Place hearts about 2cm apart on oven trays. Using 4cm heart-shaped cutter, cut out centres from hearts.
6 Bake cookies about 7 minutes; remove from oven. Reduce oven to 150°C/130°C fan-forced.
7 Divide macaroon mixture among centres of cookies; smooth surface. Cover with foil (like a tent so foil does not touch surface of macaroon). Bake about 15 minutes or until macaroon is firm. Cool on trays 5 minutes; transfer to wire racks to cool.
macaroon filling Beat egg white in small bowl with electric mixer until soft peaks form. Gradually add sugar 1 tablespoon at a time, beating until dissolved between additions. Fold in extract, coconut, flour and cherries.

prep + cook time 1 hour **makes** 22

pink macaroons

3 egg whites
2 tablespoons caster sugar
pink food colouring
1¼ cups (200g) icing sugar
1 cup (120g) ground almonds
2 tablespoons icing sugar, extra
white chocolate ganache
100g white eating chocolate, chopped coarsely
2 tablespoons thickened cream

1 Make white chocolate ganache.
2 Grease oven trays; line with baking paper.
3 Beat egg whites in small bowl with electric mixer until soft peaks form. Add sugar and food colouring, beat until sugar dissolves. Transfer mixture to large bowl. Fold in sifted icing sugar and ground almonds, in two batches.
4 Spoon mixture into large piping bag fitted with 1.5cm plain tube. Pipe 36 x 4cm rounds, 2cm apart, onto trays. Tap trays on bench top to allow macaroons to spread slightly. Dust with sifted extra icing sugar; stand 15 minutes.
5 Preheat oven to 150°C/130°C fan-forced.
6 Bake macaroons about 20 minutes. Stand macaroons on trays 5 minutes; transfer to wire rack to cool.
7 Sandwich macaroons with ganache. Dust with a little sifted icing sugar, if you like.
white chocolate ganache Stir ingredients in small saucepan over low heat until smooth. Transfer mixture to small bowl. Cover; refrigerate until ganache is spreadable.

prep + cook time 55 minutes (+ cooling) **makes** 18

amaretti

1 cup (120g) ground almonds
1 cup (220g) caster sugar
2 egg whites
¼ teaspoon almond essence
20 blanched almonds (20g)

1 Beat ground almonds, sugar, egg whites and essence in a small bowl with electric mixer 3 minutes; stand 5 minutes.
2 Spoon mixture into piping bag fitted with 1cm plain tube. Pipe onto greased oven trays in circular motion from centre out, to make biscuits about 4cm in diameter.
3 Top each biscuit with a nut. Cover loosely with foil; stand at room temperature overnight.
4 Preheat oven to 180°C/160°C fan-forced.
5 Bake biscuits about 12 minutes or until browned lightly. Stand biscuits on trays 5 minutes; transfer to wire racks to cool.

prep + cook time 40 minutes (+ standing) **makes** 20

cranberry chewies

¾ cup (60g) flaked almonds
3 egg whites
½ cup (110g) caster sugar
1 tablespoon cornflour
1 teaspoon finely grated orange rind
¾ cup (105g) dried cranberries
1 tablespoon icing sugar

1 Preheat oven to 160°C/140°C fan-forced. Grease oven trays;
line with baking paper.
2 Dry roast nuts in medium frying pan until browned lightly; remove
from pan. Cool.
3 Beat egg whites in small bowl with electric mixer until soft peaks form.
Gradually add sugar, beating until sugar dissolves. Transfer to medium
bowl; fold in sifted cornflour, rind, cranberries and nuts, in two batches.
4 Drop heaped tablespoons of mixture about 4cm apart onto trays.
5 Bake chewies about 30 minutes. Stand chewies on tray 5 minutes;
transfer to wire rack to cool. Dust with sifted icing sugar.

prep + cook time 50 minutes **makes** 18

BISCOTTI

choc nut biscotti

1 cup (220g) caster sugar
2 eggs
1⅔ cups (250g) plain flour
1 teaspoon baking powder
1 cup (150g) shelled pistachios, toasted
½ cup (70g) slivered almonds
¼ cup (25g) cocoa powder

1 Preheat oven to 180°C/160°C fan-forced. Grease oven tray.
2 Whisk sugar and eggs in medium bowl. Stir in sifted flour, baking powder and nuts; mix to a sticky dough.
3 Knead dough on floured surface until smooth. Divide into two portions; knead one portion on floured surface until smooth, but still slightly sticky. Divide this portion into four pieces. Roll each piece into 25cm log shape.
4 Knead remaining portion with cocoa until smooth. Divide into two pieces; roll each piece of chocolate mixture into a 25cm log shape.
5 Place one chocolate log on tray. Place a plain log on each side, press gently together to form a slightly flattened shape. Repeat with remaining logs.
6 Bake logs about 30 minutes or until browned lightly. Stand logs on tray 10 minutes.
7 Reduce oven to 150°C/130°C fan-forced.
8 Using a serrated knife, cut logs diagonally into 5mm slices. Place slices, in single layer, on ungreased oven trays.
9 Bake biscotti about 20 minutes or until dry and crisp, turning over halfway through cooking; cool on wire racks.

prep + cook time 1 hour 25 minutes **makes** 60

coffee and hazelnut biscotti

½ cup (110g) caster sugar
1 egg, beaten lightly
¾ cup (110g) plain flour
½ teaspoon baking powder
1 tablespoon espresso-style coffee granules
1 cup (150g) hazelnuts, roasted, chopped coarsely
100g dark eating chocolate, melted

1 Preheat oven to 180°C/160°C fan-forced. Grease oven tray.
2 Whisk sugar and egg in medium bowl. Stir in flour, baking powder and coffee and nuts; mix to a sticky dough.
3 Knead dough on floured surface until smooth. Roll dough into a 20cm log. Place on tray.
4 Bake log about 25 minutes or until browned and firm. Stand log on tray 10 minutes.
5 Reduce oven to 150°C/130°C fan-forced.
6 Using a serrated knife, cut log diagonally into 1cm slices. Place slices, in single layer, on ungreased oven tray.
7 Bake biscotti about 25 minutes or until dry and crisp, turning over halfway through cooking; cool on wire racks.
8 Spread chocolate over one side of each biscotto; leave to set at room temperature.

prep + cook time 1 hour 25 minutes (+ standing) **makes** 20

pistachio and cranberry biscotti

60g unsalted butter, softened
1 teaspoon vanilla extract
1 cup (220g) caster sugar
2 eggs
1¾ cups (260g) plain flour
½ teaspoon bicarbonate of soda
1 cup (130g) dried cranberries
¾ cup (110g) coarsely chopped roasted pistachios
1 egg, extra
1 tablespoon water
2 tablespoons caster sugar, extra

1 Beat butter, extract and sugar in medium bowl until combined. Beat in eggs, one at a time. Stir in sifted flour and soda then cranberries and nuts. Cover; refrigerate 1 hour.
2 Preheat oven to 180°C/160°C fan-forced. Grease oven tray.
3 Knead dough on floured surface until smooth but still sticky. Halve dough; shape each half into 30cm log. Place logs on oven tray.
4 Combine extra egg with the water in small bowl. Brush egg mixture over logs; sprinkle with extra sugar.
5 Bake logs about 20 minutes or until firm; cool 3 hours or overnight.
6 Preheat oven to 160°C/140°C fan-forced.
7 Using serrated knife, cut logs diagonally into 1cm slices. Place slices, in single layer, on ungreased oven trays.
8 Bake biscotti about 15 minutes or until dry and crisp, turning over halfway through cooking; cool on wire racks.

prep + cook time 1 hour (+ refrigeration & cooling) **makes** 60

aniseed biscotti

125g butter, chopped
¾ cup (165g) caster sugar
3 eggs
2 tablespoons brandy
1 tablespoon grated lemon rind
1½ cups (225g) plain flour
¾ cup (110g) self-raising flour
¾ cup (120g) blanched almonds, roasted, chopped coarsely
1 tablespoon ground aniseed

1 Beat butter and sugar in large bowl until just combined. Beat in eggs, one at a time. Add brandy and rind; mix well. Stir in flours, nuts and aniseed. Cover; refrigerate 1 hour.
2 Preheat oven to 180°C/160°C fan-forced. Grease oven tray.
3 Halve dough; shape each half into a 30cm log. Place logs on tray.
4 Bake logs about 20 minutes or until browned and firm. Stand logs on tray 10 minutes.
5 Reduce oven to 160°C/140°C fan-forced.
6 Using serrated knife, cut logs diagonally into 1cm slices. Place slices, in single layer, on ungreased oven trays.
7 Bake biscotti about 25 minutes or until dry and crisp, turning over halfway through cooking; cool on wire racks.

prep + cook time 1 hour 15 minutes (+ standing) **makes** 40

orange coconut and almond biscotti

1 cup (220g) caster sugar
2 eggs
1 teaspoon grated orange rind
1⅓ cups (200g) plain flour
⅓ cup (50g) self-raising flour
⅔ cup (50g) shredded coconut
1 cup (160g) blanched almonds

1 Preheat oven to 180°C/160°C fan-forced. Grease oven tray.
2 Whisk sugar, eggs and rind together in medium bowl. Stir in sifted flours, coconut and nuts; mix to a sticky dough.
3 Knead dough on floured surface until smooth. Halve dough; using floured hands, roll each half into a 20cm log. Place logs on tray.
4 Bake logs about 35 minutes or until browned. Cool logs on tray 10 minutes.
5 Reduce oven to 160°C/140°C fan-forced.
6 Using a serrated knife, cut logs diagonally into 1cm slices. Place slices, in single layer, on ungreased oven trays.
7 Bake biscotti about 25 minutes or until dry and crisp, turning over halfway through cooking; cool on wire racks.

prep + cook time 1 hour 25 minutes (+ cooling) **makes** 30

apricot and pine nut biscotti

1¼ cups (275g) caster sugar
2 eggs
1 teaspoon vanilla extract
1½ cups (225g) plain flour
½ cup (75g) self-raising flour
½ cup (125g) coarsely chopped glacé apricots
¼ cup (40g) pine nuts, toasted
2 teaspoons water

1 Preheat oven to 180°C/160°C fan-forced. Grease oven tray.
2 Whisk sugar, eggs and extract in medium bowl. Stir in sifted flours, apricots, pine nuts and the water; mix to a sticky dough.
3 Knead dough on floured surface until smooth. Halve dough; using floured hands, roll each half into a 30cm log. Place logs on tray.
4 Bake logs about 25 minutes or until browned. Cool on tray 10 minutes.
5 Reduce oven to 150°C/130°C fan-forced.
6 Using a serrated knife, cut logs diagonally into 1cm slices. Place slices, in single layer, on ungreased oven trays.
7 Bake biscotti about 25 minutes or until dry and crisp, turning over halfway through cooking; cool on wire racks.

prep + cook time 1 hour 15 minutes (+ cooling) **makes** 50

pistachio bread

3 egg whites
⅓ cup (75g) sugar
¼ teaspoon ground cardamom
1 teaspoon finely grated orange rind
¾ cup (110g) plain flour
¾ cup (110g) shelled pistachios

1 Preheat oven to 180°C/160°C fan-forced. Grease 8cm x 26cm bar pan; line base and sides with baking paper, extending paper 2cm above long sides of pan.
2 Beat egg whites in small bowl with electric mixer until soft peaks form. With motor operating, gradually add sugar, beating until dissolved between additions. Fold in cardamom, rind, flour and nuts; spread mixture into pan.
3 Bake pistachio bread about 30 minutes or until browned; cool in pan. Wrap in foil; stand overnight.
4 Preheat oven to 150°C/130°C fan-forced.
5 Using a serrated knife, cut bread on an angle into 3mm slices. Place slices on ungreased oven trays.
6 Bake slices about 15 minutes or until crisp and dry; transfer to wire rack to cool.

prep + cook time 55 minutes (+ standing & cooling) **makes** 35

chocolate almond bread

2 egg whites
1/3 cup (75g) caster sugar
3/4 cup (110g) plain flour
1 tablespoon cocoa powder
3/4 cup (120g) blanched almonds, roasted

1 Preheat oven to 180°C/160°C fan-forced. Grease 8cm x 26cm bar cake pan; line base and sides with baking paper, extending paper 2cm above long sides of pan.
2 Beat egg whites in small bowl with electric mixer until soft peaks form; gradually add sugar, beating until sugar is dissolved between additions. Fold in combined sifted flour and cocoa powder, then almonds; spread mixture into pan.
3 Bake almond bread about 25 minutes or until browned; cool in pan. Wrap in foil; stand overnight.
4 Preheat oven to 150°C/130°C fan-forced.
5 Using a serrated knife, cut bread into 3mm slices. Place slices, in a single layer, on ungreased oven trays.
6 Bake slices about 20 minutes or until crisp and dry; transfer to wire racks to cool.

prep + cook time 1 hour (+ standing & cooling) **makes** 70

pistachio almond crisps

3 egg whites
½ cup (110g) caster sugar
pinch ground cardamom
1 cup (150g) plain flour
½ cup (80g) blanched almonds
½ cup (70g) roasted unsalted pistachios

1 Preheat oven to 160°C/140°C fan-forced. Grease 30cm-square piece of foil.
2 Beat egg whites in small bowl with electric mixer until soft peaks form. Gradually add sugar, beating until dissolved between additions. Transfer mixture to medium bowl. Fold in sifted dry ingredients and nuts.
3 Spoon mixture onto foil, shape into 7cm x 25cm log. Enclose firmly in foil; place on oven tray.
4 Bake log about 45 minutes or until firm. Turn log out of foil onto wire rack to cool.
5 Reduce oven to 120°C/100°C fan-forced.
6 Using serrated knife, cut log into thin slices. Place slices in single layer on oven trays.
7 Bake about 20 minutes or until crisp; transfer to wire racks to cool.

prep + cook time 1 hour 20 minutes (+ cooling) **makes** 65

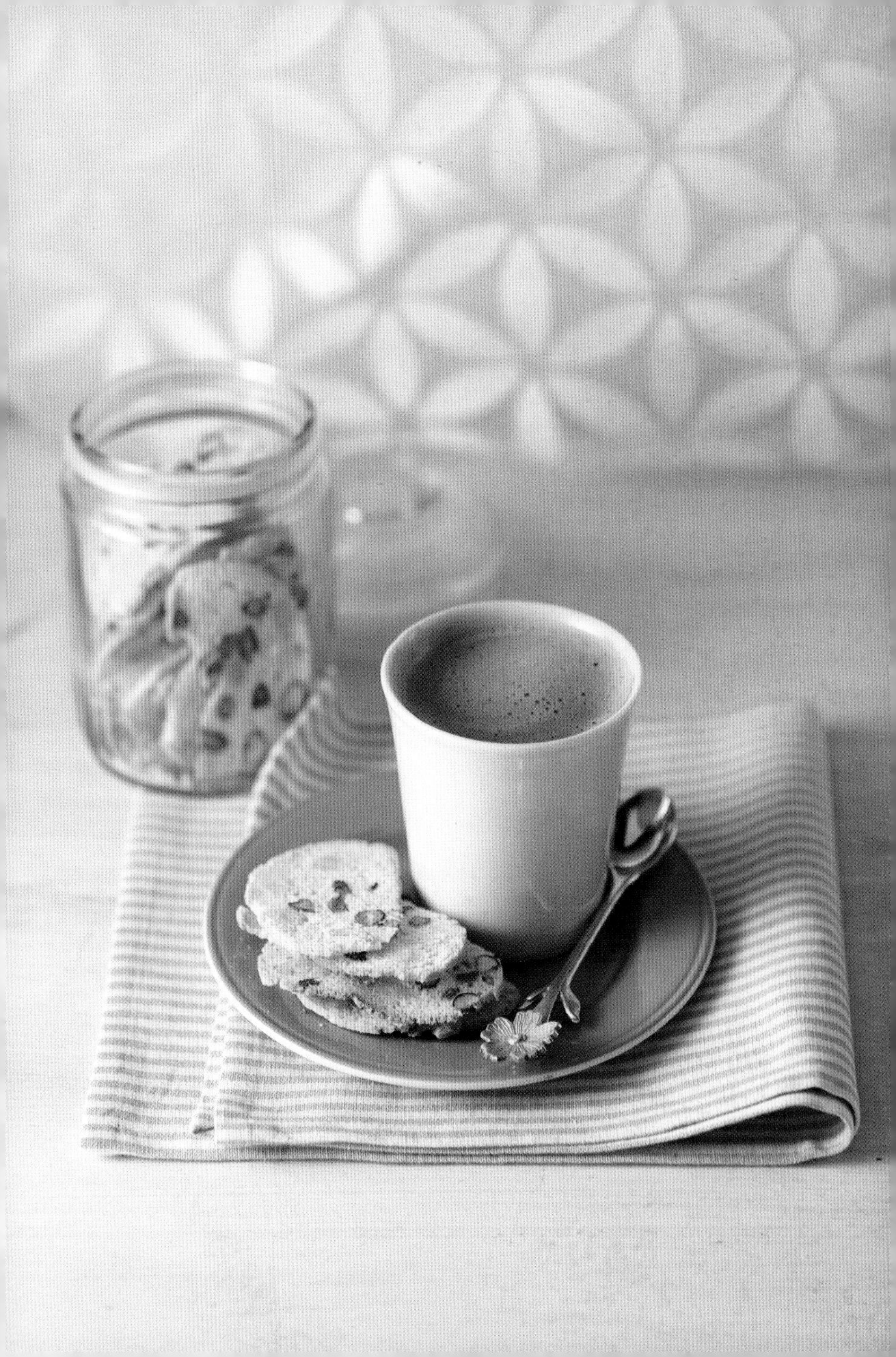

lemon grass, ginger and sesame bread

You will need eight 40g packets of original sesame snaps for this recipe.

125g butter, softened
⅔ cup (130g) firmly packed grated palm sugar
½ teaspoon ground cardamom
½ teaspoon ground cinnamon
pinch ground nutmeg
pinch ground clove
2 egg yolks
1½ cups (225g) plain flour
10cm stick (20g) fresh lemon grass, chopped finely
2 tablespoons finely chopped glacé ginger
32 sesame snaps

1 Beat butter, sugar, spices and egg yolks in small bowl with electric mixer until smooth. Stir in sifted flour, lemon grass and ginger.
2 Knead dough on floured surface until smooth. Roll dough between sheets of baking paper until 5mm thick. Refrigerate 30 minutes.
3 Preheat oven to 160°C/140°C fan-forced. Grease oven trays; line with baking paper.
4 Using 9cm square cutter, cut 16 shapes from dough; cut in half to make 32 rectangles. Place about 5cm apart on oven trays.
5 Bake biscuits 12 minutes.
6 Carefully trim edges of sesame snaps to fit the top of each biscuit. Top each hot biscuit with a sesame snap; bake 3 minutes. Cool on trays.

prep + cook time 40 minutes (+ refrigeration) **makes** 32

SLICES

chocolate caramel slice

¾ cup (110g) plain flour
⅓ cup (25g) desiccated coconut
⅓ cup (75g) firmly packed brown sugar
90g butter, melted
395g can sweetened condensed milk
60g butter, extra
2 tablespoons maple syrup
200g dark eating chocolate, chopped coarsely
2 teaspoons vegetable oil

1 Preheat oven to 170°C/150°C fan-forced. Grease shallow 22cm-square cake pan; line with baking paper, extending paper 5cm above sides.
2 Combine sifted flour, coconut, sugar and butter in medium bowl; press mixture firmly over base of pan.
3 Bake base about 15 minutes or until browned lightly; cool.
4 Meanwhile, stir condensed milk, extra butter and syrup in small saucepan over medium heat until smooth.
5 Pour caramel mixture over base; bake 25 minutes. Cool.
6 Stir chocolate and oil in small saucepan over low heat until smooth. Pour chocolate over caramel. Refrigerate slice about 3 hours or until set before cutting.

prep + cook time 45 minutes (+ refrigeration) **makes** 16

lime coconut slice

90g butter, softened
½ cup (110g) caster sugar
1 egg
⅓ cup (50g) self-raising flour
¾ cup (110g) plain flour
1 cup (340g) lime marmalade
coconut topping
2 eggs
¼ cup (55g) caster sugar
2 cups (150g) shredded coconut
1 cup (80g) desiccated coconut

1 Preheat oven to 180°C/160°C fan-forced. Grease 19cm x 30cm lamington pan; line with baking paper, extending paper 5cm over long sides.
2 Beat butter, sugar and egg in small bowl with electric mixer until light and fluffy; stir in sifted flours. Press dough into pan; spread with marmalade.
3 Meanwhile, make coconut topping; sprinkle over marmalade.
4 Bake slice about 45 minutes; cool in pan.
coconut topping Whisk eggs and sugar in medium bowl; stir in coconuts.

prep + cook time 1 hour **makes** 20

muesli slice

125g butter, chopped coarsely
⅓ cup (75g) firmly packed brown sugar
2 tablespoons honey
1⅓ cups (120g) rolled oats
½ cup (40g) shredded coconut
½ cup (75g) self-raising flour
½ cup (65g) dried cranberries
½ cup (80g) finely chopped dried pineapple
½ cup (70g) slivered almonds
2 tablespoons pepitas

1 Preheat oven to 180°C/160°C fan-forced. Grease 19cm x 30cm lamington pan; line with baking paper, extending paper 5cm over long sides.
2 Stir butter, sugar and honey in medium saucepan over heat until sugar dissolves. Stir in remaining ingredients. Press mixture firmly into pan.
3 Bake slice about 20 minutes. Cool in pan before cutting.

prep + cook time 40 minutes **makes** 30

fruit mince slice

¾ cup (110g) plain flour
½ cup (75g) self-raising flour
2 tablespoons caster sugar
100g cold butter, chopped coarsely
1 egg yolk
1 tablespoon milk
410g jar fruit mince
2 large apples (400g), peeled, grated coarsely
1 sheet puff pastry
1 egg yolk, extra

1 Grease 19cm x 30cm lamington pan; line with baking paper, extending paper 5cm over long sides.
2 Sift flours and sugar into large bowl; rub in butter then stir in egg yolk and milk. Knead dough on floured surface until smooth. Cover; refrigerate 30 minutes.
3 Preheat oven to 200°C/180°C fan-forced.
4 Roll dough between sheets of baking paper until large enough to cover base of pan; press into pan. Spread combined fruit mince and apple over dough.
5 Cut puff pastry into 2cm-wide strips; place strips over filling in a lattice pattern. Brush pastry with a little extra egg yolk.
6 Bake slice about 30 minutes. Cool in pan before cutting.

prep + cook time 1 hour (+ refrigeration) **makes** 18

butterscotch peanut slice

150g butter, chopped coarsely
¾ cup (165g) firmly packed brown sugar
¼ cup (60ml) cream
1 cup (150g) plain flour
⅓ cup (50g) self-raising flour
2 eggs
¼ cup (35g) coarsely chopped roasted unsalted peanuts
butterscotch icing
30g butter
¼ cup (55g) brown sugar
1 tablespoon milk
½ cup (80g) icing sugar

1 Preheat oven to 170°C/150°C fan-forced. Grease shallow 22cm-square cake pan; line with baking paper, extending paper 5cm over sides.
2 Stir butter, sugar and cream in medium saucepan over heat until sugar dissolves; bring to the boil. Reduce heat; simmer, uncovered, 2 minutes. Cool 10 minutes.
3 Stir sifted flours, eggs and nuts into butter mixture; spread mixture into pan.
4 Bake slice about 25 minutes. Stand slice in pan 5 minutes; turn, top-side up, onto wire rack to cool.
5 Meanwhile, make butterscotch icing.
6 Spread icing over slice, leave to set before cutting.
butterscotch icing Stir butter, sugar and milk in small saucepan over low heat until smooth; bring to the boil. Remove from heat; stir in sifted icing sugar.

prep + cook time 35 minutes **makes** 16

chocolate freckle slice

185g butter, softened
220g jar chocolate hazelnut spread
⅓ cup (75g) firmly packed brown sugar
1¾ cups (260g) plain flour
200g packet freckles

1 Preheat oven to 160°C/140°C fan-forced. Grease 19cm x 30cm lamington pan; line with baking paper, extending paper 5cm over long sides.
2 Beat butter, spread and sugar in small bowl with electric mixer until combined. Stir in sifted flour, in two batches.
3 Press dough into pan; smooth surface with spatula.
4 Bake slice 25 minutes. Remove pan from oven; working quickly, press freckles firmly onto slice in rows about 1.5cm apart. Cool slice in pan; cut when cold.

prep + cook time 45 minutes **makes** 35

choc peanut butter squares

¾ cup (210g) smooth peanut butter
50g unsalted butter, softened
¼ cup (55g) firmly packed dark brown sugar
1 cup (160g) icing sugar
250g milk eating chocolate, chopped coarsely
¼ cup (35g) roasted crushed peanuts

1 Preheat oven to 180°C/160°C fan-forced. Grease deep 20cm-square loose-based cake pan.
2 Combine peanut butter, butter, brown sugar and sifted icing sugar in medium bowl; press mixture evenly over base of pan.
3 Bake slice 10 minutes.
4 Meanwhile, stir chocolate and nuts in small saucepan over low heat until chocolate is melted.
5 Pour chocolate mixture over base. Refrigerate 3 hours or overnight until set.

prep + cook time 25 minutes (+ refrigeration) **makes** 36

white chocolate macadamia slice

125g butter, chopped coarsely
180g white eating chocolate, chopped coarsely
½ cup (110g) caster sugar
2 eggs
1 cup (150g) plain flour
½ cup (75g) self-raising flour
¾ cup (105g) coarsely chopped roasted macadamias
¾ cup (135g) white Choc Bits
1 tablespoon icing sugar

1 Preheat oven to 160°C/140°C fan-forced. Grease 19cm x 30cm lamington pan; line with baking paper, extending paper 5cm over long sides.
2 Stir butter and chocolate in medium saucepan over low heat until smooth. Cool 10 minutes.
3 Stir sugar and eggs into chocolate mixture, then sifted flours, nuts and Choc Bits. Spread mixture into pan.
4 Bake slice about 30 minutes. Cool slice in pan. Dust with sifted icing sugar before serving.

prep + cook time 50 minutes **makes** 20

pineapple coconut slice

185g butter, softened
¾ cup (165g) caster sugar
3 eggs
⅔ cup (50g) desiccated coconut
1¾ cups (260g) self-raising flour
270ml can coconut cream
440g can crushed pineapple, well-drained
⅓ cup (25g) shredded coconut
lime glacé icing
1½ cups (240g) icing sugar
20g butter, melted
2 tablespoons lime juice, approximately

1 Preheat oven to 180°C/160°C fan-forced. Grease 22cm x 32cm rectangular cake pan; line with baking paper, extending paper 5cm over long sides.
2 Beat butter and sugar in small bowl with electric mixer until light and fluffy. Beat in eggs, one at a time. Transfer mixture to large bowl; stir in coconut, sifted flour, coconut cream and pineapple, in two batches. Spread mixture into pan.
3 Bake cake 45 minutes. Stand cake in pan 10 minutes; turn, top-side up, onto wire rack to cool.
4 Meanwhile, make lime glacé icing.
5 Spread icing over cake, sprinkle with coconut.
lime glacé icing Sift icing sugar into small heatproof bowl; stir in butter and enough of the juice to make a soft paste. Stir over small saucepan of simmering water until icing is spreadable.

prep + cook time 1 hour **makes** 20

triple chocolate slice

250g plain chocolate biscuits
325g dark eating chocolate, chopped coarsely
200g butter, chopped coarsely
3 eggs
3 egg yolks
⅓ cup (75g) caster sugar
1 tablespoon cocoa powder

1 Preheat oven to 160°C/140°C fan-forced. Grease 19cm x 30cm
lamington pan; line with baking paper, extending paper 5cm over
long sides.
2 Place biscuits in a single layer over base of pan; trim to fit if necessary.
3 Stir chocolate and butter in medium saucepan over low heat until
smooth. Remove from heat.
4 Beat eggs, egg yolks and sugar in medium bowl with electric mixer
until thick and creamy; beat in warm chocolate mixture. Pour mixture
over biscuits.
5 Bake slice about 25 minutes or until filling is set. Cool slice in pan
15 minutes; refrigerate 1 hour. Dust with sifted cocoa before cutting.

prep + cook time 40 minutes (+ refrigeration) **makes** 30

date slice

1½ cups (225g) plain flour
1¼ cups (185g) self-raising flour
150g butter, chopped coarsely
1 tablespoon honey
1 egg
⅓ cup (80ml) milk, approximately
1 tablespoon white sugar
date filling
3½ cups (500g) dried seeded dates, chopped coarsely
¾ cup (180ml) water
2 tablespoons finely grated lemon rind
2 tablespoons lemon juice

1 Make date filling.
2 Grease 20cm x 30cm lamington pan; line with baking paper, extending paper 5cm over long sides.
3 Sift flours into medium bowl; rub in butter using fingertips. Stir in honey, egg and enough milk to make a firm dough. Knead on floured surface until smooth. Enclose with plastic wrap; refrigerate 30 minutes.
4 Preheat oven to 200°C/180°C fan-forced.
5 Divide dough in half. Roll one half large enough to cover base of pan; ease into pan. Spread filling over dough. Roll remaining dough large enough to cover filling; place over filling. Brush dough with a little milk; sprinkle with sugar.
6 Bake slice about 20 minutes; cool in pan before cutting.
date filling Cook ingredients in medium saucepan, stirring, about 10 minutes or until thick and smooth. Cool.

prep + cook time 1 hour 25 minutes (+ refrigeration) **makes** 24

triple choc cheesecake slice

24 (310g) chocolate-chip cookies
½ cup (125ml) thickened cream
250g white eating chocolate, chopped coarsely
500g soft cream cheese
¾ cup (165g) caster sugar
2 eggs
chocolate ganache
200g dark eating chocolate, chopped coarsely
⅓ cup (80ml) cream

1 Preheat oven to 150°C/130°C fan-forced. Grease 19cm x 30cm lamington pan; line with baking paper, extending paper 5cm over long sides.
2 Place cookies in single layer over base of pan; trim to fit if necessary.
3 Stir cream and chocolate in small saucepan over low heat until smooth. Cool.
4 Beat cream cheese and sugar in medium bowl with electric mixer until smooth. Beat in eggs, one at a time; beat in chocolate mixture. Pour mixture into pan.
5 Bake slice about 35 minutes or until set. Cool in oven with door ajar. Refrigerate 3 hours or overnight.
6 Make chocolate ganache; spread over cheesecake. Refrigerate until set.
7 Remove cheesecake from pan; remove paper from base before cutting.
chocolate ganache Stir ingredients in small pan over low heat until smooth; cool 15 minutes.

prep + cook time 50 minutes (+ cooling & refrigeration) **makes** 24

choc-mint slice

1 cup (220g) caster sugar
⅔ cup (160ml) evaporated milk
2 teaspoons glucose syrup
15g butter
100g white marshmallows, chopped coarsely
400g dark eating chocolate, chopped coarsely
peppermint oil or essence

1 Grease 19cm x 29cm slice pan; line with baking paper, extending paper 5cm over long sides.
2 Stir sugar, milk, glucose and butter in medium heavy-based saucepan over heat, without boiling, until sugar dissolves. Bring to the boil; boil, stirring, about 4 minutes or until mixture becomes the colour of creamed honey and begins to catch on the base of the pan.
3 Remove pan from heat; quickly stir in marshmallows and 250g of the chocolate. Flavour mixture with oil or essence to taste. Spread mixture into pan.
4 Working quickly, melt remaining chocolate in small heatproof bowl over small saucepan of simmering water; spread chocolate over slice. Refrigerate choc-mint slice until set before cutting.

prep + cook time 30 minutes (+ refrigeration) **makes** 36

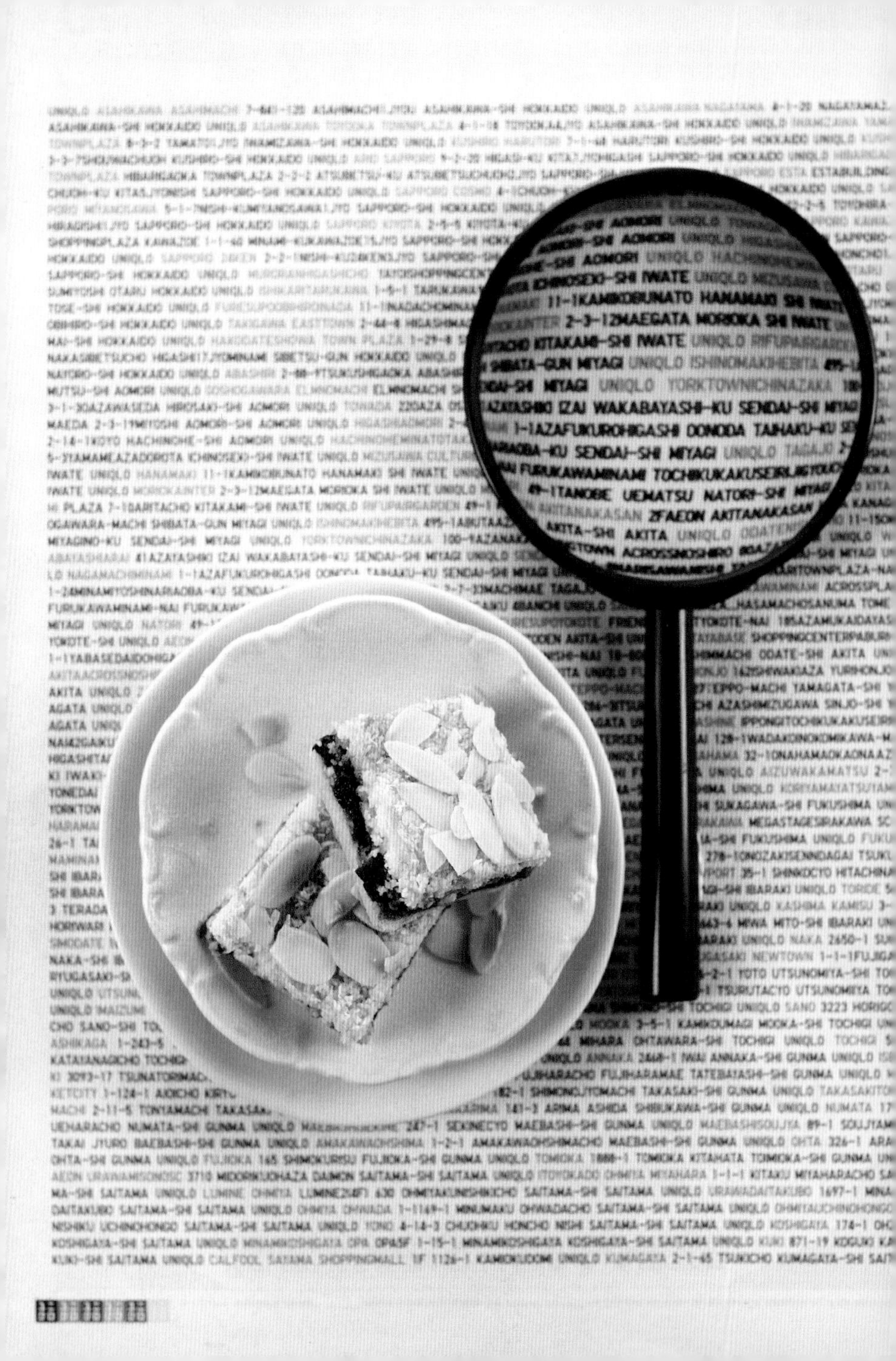

cherry almond coconut slice

60g butter, softened
⅓ cup (75g) caster sugar
1 egg yolk
2 tablespoons self-raising flour
½ cup (75g) plain flour
⅔ cup (220g) cherry jam
1 tablespoon cherry brandy
⅓ cup (25g) flaked almonds
topping
2 eggs
¼ cup (55g) caster sugar
2 cups (160g) desiccated coconut

1 Preheat oven to 180°C/160°C fan-forced. Grease 19cm x 29cm slice pan; line with baking paper, extending paper 5cm over long sides.
2 Beat butter, sugar and egg yolk in small bowl with electric mixer until light and fluffy. Stir in sifted flours. Press mixture into pan; spread with combined jam and brandy.
3 Make topping; sprinkle over slice. Sprinkle with nuts; press down gently.
4 Bake slice about 30 minutes; cool in pan before cutting.
topping Beat eggs and sugar with fork in medium bowl; stir in coconut.

prep + cook time 50 minutes **makes** 20

white chocolate and glacé fruit slice

½ cup (70g) roasted unsalted pistachios
¼ cup (50g) halved green glacé cherries
¼ cup (50g) halved red glacé cherries
¼ cup (60g) coarsely chopped glacé peaches
¼ cup (55g) coarsely chopped glacé ginger
200g white eating chocolate, melted

1 Grease 8cm x 26cm bar cake pan; line with baking paper, extending paper 5cm over long sides.
2 Combine nuts, fruits and ginger in medium bowl. Working quickly, stir in chocolate; spread mixture into pan, push down firmly to flatten.
3 Refrigerate slice until set. Turn bar onto board, cut into slices.

prep + cook time 25 minutes (+ refrigeration) **makes** 16

vanilla slice

1 sheet puff pastry
¼ cup (55g) caster sugar
¼ cup (35g) cornflour
1 ½ tablespoons custard powder
1 ¼ cups (310ml) milk
30g butter
1 egg yolk
½ teaspoon vanilla extract
passionfruit icing
¾ cup (110g) icing sugar
1 tablespoon passionfruit pulp
1 teaspoon water, approximately

1 Preheat oven to 240°C/220°C fan-forced. Grease 8cm x 26cm bar cake pan; line with strip of foil extending over long sides of pan.
2 Place pastry sheet on oven tray. Bake about 15 minutes or until puffed; cool. Split pastry in half horizontally; remove and discard any uncooked pastry from centre. Flatten pastry pieces gently with hand; trim both to fit pan. Place top half in pan, top-side down.
3 Meanwhile, combine sugar, cornflour and custard powder in medium saucepan; gradually stir in milk. Stir over heat until mixture boils and thickens. Reduce heat; simmer, stirring, about 3 minutes or until custard is thick and smooth. Remove pan from heat; stir in butter, egg yolk and extract.
4 Spread hot custard over pastry in pan; top with remaining pastry, bottom-side up, press down gently. Cool to room temperature.
5 Meanwhile, make passionfruit icing.
6 Spread pastry with icing; set at room temperature. Refrigerate 3 hours before cutting.
passionfruit icing Sift icing sugar into small heatproof bowl; stir in passionfruit and enough water to make a thick paste. Stir over small saucepan of simmering water until icing is spreadable.

prep + cook time 45 minutes (+ refrigeration) **makes** 8

choc-chip, fig and pecan slice

185g unsalted butter, softened
¾ cup (165g) firmly packed brown sugar
1¼ cups (185g) plain flour
⅓ cup (65g) finely chopped dried figs
½ cup (60g) finely chopped roasted pecans
½ cup (95g) dark Choc Bits
100g dark eating chocolate, melted

1 Preheat oven to 180°C/160°C fan-forced. Grease 20cm x 30cm lamington pan; line with baking paper, extending paper 5cm over long sides.
2 Beat butter and sugar in small bowl with electric mixer until light and fluffy. Stir in sifted flour, then figs, nuts and Choc Bits. Press mixture into pan.
3 Bake slice about 25 minutes. Mark slice into 24 squares; cool in pan. Drizzle slice with chocolate; cut into squares when chocolate is set.

prep + cook time 45 minutes (+ cooling) **makes** 24

black forest slice

2 eggs
2 egg yolks
⅓ cup (75g) caster sugar
85g dark eating chocolate, melted
1 cup (250ml) milk
1 cup (250ml) cream
1 cup (120g) ground almonds
¼ cup (35g) plain flour
1 tablespoon cocoa powder
425g can seeded black cherries, drained
85g dark eating chocolate, grated coarsely

1 Preheat oven to 180°C/160°C fan-forced. Grease 23cm-square slab cake pan.
2 Beat eggs, egg yolks and sugar in medium bowl with electric mixer until combined; beat in cooled chocolate. Beat in milk and cream on low speed. Stir in ground almonds, then sifted flour and cocoa. Pour mixture into pan; sprinkle with cherries and grated chocolate.
3 Bake slice about 25 minutes. Stand slice in pan 15 minutes; turn, top-side up, onto wire rack to cool.

prep + cook time 45 minutes (+ standing) **makes** 20

iced coconut slice

4 egg yolks
2 tablespoons caster sugar
100g white eating chocolate, melted
⅓ cup (80ml) coconut-flavoured liqueur
2 egg whites
300ml cream, whipped
1 small pineapple (900g), peeled, cored, chopped finely
½ cup finely shredded fresh mint
½ cup (125ml) pineapple juice

1 Line 14cm x 21cm loaf pan with strips of foil, extending foil 10cm over sides of pan.
2 Beat egg yolks and sugar in small bowl with electric mixer until thick and creamy; transfer to large bowl. Stir in chocolate and liqueur.
3 Beat egg whites in small bowl with electric mixer until soft peaks form. Fold egg whites and cream into chocolate mixture, in two batches.
4 Pour mixture into pan; cover with foil, freeze overnight until firm.
5 Combine remaining ingredients in small bowl.
6 Serve pieces of slice topped with pineapple mixture.

prep + cook time 30 minutes (+ freezing) **makes** 10

decadent double-choc slice

250g dark eating chocolate, melted
1¼ cups (135g) coarsely chopped roasted walnuts
150g dark eating chocolate, chopped coarsely
¾ cup (165g) firmly packed brown sugar
3 eggs

1 Grease 19cm x 29cm slice pan; line base and long sides with foil, extending foil 5cm over sides.
2 Spread melted chocolate over base of pan; refrigerate until set.
3 Preheat oven to 180°C/160°C fan-forced.
4 Process nuts, chopped chocolate, sugar and eggs until combined. Pour nut mixture over chocolate base.
5 Bake slice about 20 minutes; cool in pan. Remove from pan; carefully remove foil. Cut into squares.

prep + cook time 45 minutes (+ refrigeration & cooling) **makes** 24

jewelled rocky road

300g toasted marshmallows with coconut, chopped coarsely
½ cup (40g) flaked almonds, roasted
4 slices glacé pineapple (125g), chopped coarsely
½ cup (125g) coarsely chopped glacé peaches
½ cup (100g) coarsely chopped glacé citron
450g white eating chocolate, melted

1 Grease 19cm x 29cm slice pan; line with baking paper, extending paper 5cm over long sides.
2 Combine marshmallows, nuts and fruit in large bowl. Working quickly, stir in chocolate; spread mixture into pan, pushing down firmly to flatten.
3 Refrigerate rocky road until set before cutting into squares.

prep + cook time 25 minutes (+ refrigeration) **makes** 35

hedgehog slice

¾ cup (180ml) sweetened condensed milk
60g butter
125g dark eating chocolate, chopped coarsely
150g plain sweet biscuits
⅓ cup (45g) roasted unsalted peanuts
⅓ cup (55g) sultanas

1 Grease 8cm x 26cm bar pan; line with baking paper, extending paper 5cm over long sides.
2 Stir condensed milk and butter in small saucepan over low heat until smooth. Remove from heat; stir in chocolate until smooth.
3 Break biscuits into small pieces; place in large bowl with nuts and sultanas. Add chocolate mixture; stir to combine.
4 Spread mixture into pan. Cover; refrigerate about 4 hours or until firm. Remove from pan; cut into slices.

prep + cook time 25 minutes (+ refrigeration) **makes** 12

raspberry coconut slice

90g butter
½ cup (110g) caster sugar
1 egg
¼ cup (35g) self-raising flour
⅔ cup (100g) plain flour
1 tablespoon custard powder
⅔ cup (220g) raspberry jam
coconut topping
2 cups (160g) desiccated coconut
¼ cup (55g) caster sugar
2 eggs, beaten lightly

1 Preheat oven to 180°C/160°C fan-forced. Grease 20cm x 30cm lamington pan; line with baking paper, extending paper 5cm over long sides.
2 Beat butter, sugar and egg in small bowl with electric mixer until light and fluffy. Transfer to medium bowl; stir in sifted flours and custard powder. Spread dough into pan; spread with jam.
3 Make coconut topping; sprinkle over jam.
4 Bake slice about 40 minutes; cool in pan.
coconut topping Combine ingredients in small bowl.

prep + cook time 55 minutes (+ cooling) **makes** 16

choc-peppermint slice

250g plain sweet biscuits
100g butter, chopped
½ cup (125ml) sweetened condensed milk
2 x 35g Peppermint Crisp chocolate bars, chopped coarsely
chocolate topping
200g milk eating chocolate, chopped coarsely
2 teaspoons vegetable oil

1 Grease 19cm x 29cm slice pan; line with baking paper, extending paper 5cm over long sides.
2 Process 200g of the biscuits until fine. Chop remaining biscuits coarsely.
3 Stir butter and milk in small saucepan over low heat until smooth.
4 Combine processed and chopped biscuits with chocolate bar in medium bowl; stir in butter mixture. Press mixture firmly into pan; refrigerate, covered, about 20 minutes or until set.
5 Meanwhile, make chocolate topping; spread over slice.
6 Refrigerate slice until firm before cutting into 24 squares.
chocolate topping Stir ingredients in small heatproof bowl over small saucepan of simmering water until smooth.

prep + cook time 20 minutes (+ refrigeration) **makes** 24

apricot and coconut slice

250g plain sweet biscuits
100g butter, chopped
½ cup (125ml) sweetened condensed milk
½ cup (40g) toasted shredded coconut
½ cup (80g) finely chopped dried apricots
chocolate topping
200g white eating chocolate, chopped coarsely
2 teaspoons vegetable oil

1 Grease 19cm x 29cm slice pan; line with baking paper, extending paper 5cm over long sides.
2 Process 200g of the biscuits until fine. Chop remaining biscuits coarsely.
3 Stir butter and milk in small saucepan over low heat until smooth.
4 Combine processed and chopped biscuits with coconut and apricots in medium bowl; stir in butter mixture. Press mixture firmly into pan; refrigerate, covered, about 20 minutes or until set.
5 Meanwhile, make chocolate topping; spread over slice.
6 Refrigerate slice until firm before cutting into 24 squares.
chocolate topping Stir ingredients in small heatproof bowl over small saucepan of simmering water until smooth.

prep + cook time 20 minutes (+ refrigeration) **makes** 24

lemon slice

250g plain sweet biscuits
100g butter, chopped
½ cup (125ml) sweetened condensed milk
1 teaspoon finely grated lemon rind
1 tablespoon lemon juice
lemon icing
1¼ cups (200g) icing sugar
10g butter
1 tablespoon lemon juice

1 Grease 19cm x 29cm slice pan; line with baking paper, extending paper 5cm over long sides.
2 Process 200g of the biscuits until fine. Chop remaining biscuits coarsely.
3 Stir butter, milk, rind and juice in small saucepan over low heat until smooth. Remove from heat.
4 Combine processed and chopped biscuits in medium bowl; stir in butter mixture. Press mixture firmly into pan; refrigerate, covered, about 20 minutes or until set.
5 Meanwhile, make lemon icing; spread over slice.
6 Refrigerate slice until firm before cutting into 24 squares.
lemon icing Stir ingredients in small heatproof bowl over small saucepan of simmering water until smooth.

prep + cook time 20 minutes (+ refrigeration) **makes** 24

berry sponge slice

2 sheets sweet puff pastry, thawed
3 eggs
½ cup (110g) caster sugar
½ cup (75g) self-raising flour
1½ cups (225g) frozen mixed berries
1 egg white, beaten lightly
1 tablespoon caster sugar, extra
1 tablespoon icing sugar

1 Preheat oven to 220°C/200°C fan-forced. Grease 25cm x 30cm swiss roll pan.
2 Roll one pastry sheet until large enough to cover base of pan, extending pastry halfway up sides. Prick pastry with fork at 2cm intervals; freeze 5 minutes.
3 Place another swiss roll pan on top of pastry; bake 5 minutes. Remove top pan; bake further 5 minutes or until pastry is browned lightly. Cool 5 minutes.
4 Meanwhile, beat whole eggs and sugar in small bowl with electric mixer until thick and creamy; fold in sifted flour. Spread mixture evenly over pastry; sprinkle evenly with berries.
5 Roll remaining pastry sheet large enough to fit pan; place over berries. Brush pastry with egg white, sprinkle with extra sugar; score pastry in crosshatch pattern.
6 Bake slice about 20 minutes. Cool in pan; dust with sifted icing sugar then cut into squares.

prep + cook time 50 minutes **makes** 20

lemon meringue slice

90g butter, softened
2 tablespoons caster sugar
1 egg
1 cup (150g) plain flour
¼ cup (80g) apricot jam
lemon topping
2 eggs
2 egg yolks
½ cup (110g) caster sugar
300ml cream
1 tablespoon finely grated lemon rind
2 tablespoons lemon juice
meringue
3 egg whites
¾ cup (165g) caster sugar

1 Preheat oven to 200°C/180°C fan-forced. Grease 19cm x 29cm slice pan; line with baking paper, extending paper 5cm over long sides.
2 Beat butter, sugar and egg in small bowl with electric mixer until pale in colour; stir in sifted flour, in two batches. Press dough over base of pan; prick dough all over with a fork.
3 Bake base about 15 minutes or until browned lightly. Cool 20 minutes; spread base with jam. Reduce oven to 170°C/150°C fan-forced.
4 Make lemon topping; pour over base. Bake about 35 minutes or until set; cool 20 minutes. Roughen surface of topping with fork.
5 Increase oven to 220°C/200°C fan-forced.
6 Make meringue; spread evenly over topping.
7 Bake slice about 3 minutes or until browned lightly. Cool slice in pan 20 minutes before cutting.
lemon topping Whisk ingredients in medium bowl until combined.
meringue Beat egg whites in small bowl with electric mixer until soft peaks form; gradually add sugar, beating until dissolved between additions.

prep + cook time 1 hour 20 minutes (+ cooling) **makes** 16

apple and prune slice

4 medium apples (600g)
¾ cup (135g) coarsely chopped seeded prunes
2½ cups (625ml) water
½ teaspoon ground cinnamon
½ teaspoon ground nutmeg
2 tablespoons ground hazelnuts
2 sheets shortcrust pastry, thawed
1 tablespoon caster sugar

1 Peel and core apples; slice thinly. Place apples, prunes and the water in medium saucepan; bring to the boil. Reduce heat; simmer, covered, 10 minutes or until apples are just tender. Drain well; cool 15 minutes.
2 Combine spices and ground hazelnuts in medium bowl; gently stir in apple mixture.
3 Preheat oven to 200°C/180°C fan-forced. Grease 20cm x 30cm lamington pan; line base with baking paper.
4 Roll one pastry sheet large enough to cover base of pan; place in pan, trim edges. Cover pastry with baking paper, fill with dried beans or uncooked rice; bake 15 minutes. Remove paper and beans; bake further 5 minutes. Spread apple mixture over pastry.
5 Roll remaining pastry sheet large enough to fit pan; place over apple filling. Brush pastry with a little water, sprinkle with sugar; score pastry in crosshatch pattern.
6 Bake slice about 45 minutes. Cool in pan; cut into squares.

prep + cook time 1 hour 30 minutes (+ cooling) **makes** 24

dutch ginger and almond slice

1¾ cups (255g) plain flour
1 cup (220g) caster sugar
⅔ cup (150g) coarsely chopped glacé ginger
½ cup (80g) coarsely chopped blanched almonds
1 egg
185g butter, melted
2 teaspoons icing sugar

1 Preheat oven to 180°C/160°C fan-forced. Grease 20cm x 30cm lamington pan; line with baking paper, extending paper 5cm over long sides.
2 Combine sifted flour, sugar, ginger, nuts and egg in medium bowl; stir in butter. Press mixture into pan. Mark slice into squares or rectangles.
3 Bake slice about 35 minutes. Stand slice in pan 10 minutes; cut into squares or rectangles, transfer to wire rack to cool. Dust with sifted icing sugar.

prep + cook time 50 minutes **makes** 20

chocolate hazelnut slice

250g plain chocolate biscuits
60g butter, melted
4 eggs, separated
¾ cup (165g) caster sugar
½ cup (50g) ground hazelnuts
2 tablespoons plain flour
topping
125g butter, softened
½ cup (110g) caster sugar
1 tablespoon orange juice
200g dark eating chocolate, melted
1 tablespoon cocoa powder

1 Preheat oven to 180°C/160°C fan-forced. Grease 20cm x 30cm
lamington pan; line with baking paper, extending paper 2cm over long sides.
2 Process biscuits until fine. Combine 1 cup of the biscuit crumbs with
butter in medium bowl; press over base of pan. Refrigerate 10 minutes.
3 Beat egg whites in small bowl with electric mixer until soft peaks form.
Gradually add sugar, beating until dissolved between additions; fold in
ground hazelnuts, remaining biscuit crumbs and sifted flour. Spread
mixture over biscuit base.
4 Bake base about 20 minutes. Cool 20 minutes.
5 Reduce oven to170°C/150°C fan-forced.
6 Meanwhile, make topping by beating butter, sugar, egg yolks and juice
in small bowl with electric mixer until light and fluffy. Stir in chocolate.
Spread topping over slice.
7 Bake slice about 20 minutes; cool in pan. Refrigerate until firm; dust
with sifted cocoa before cutting.

prep + cook time 1 hour 10 minutes (+ cooling & refrigeration)
makes 24

cranberry and muesli slice

125g butter
⅓ cup (75g) firmly packed brown sugar
2 tablespoons honey
1½ cups (135g) rolled oats
½ cup (75g) self-raising flour
1 cup (130g) dried cranberries
1 cup (140g) roasted shelled pistachios, chopped coarsely

1 Preheat oven to 180°C/160°C fan-forced. Grease 20cm x 30cm lamington pan; line with baking paper, extending paper 2cm over two long sides.
2 Melt butter with sugar and honey in medium saucepan over medium heat without boiling, stirring, until sugar is dissolved. Stir in remaining ingredients. Press mixture firmly into pan.
3 Bake slice about 20 minutes. Cool in pan before cutting.

prep + cook time 40 minutes **makes** 30

cherry friand slice

4 egg whites
100g butter, melted
1 tablespoon milk
½ teaspoon vanilla extract
1 cup (120g) ground almonds
1 cup (160g) icing sugar
⅓ cup (50g) self-raising flour
1 vanilla bean
⅔ cup (100g) frozen cherries, chopped coarsely

1 Preheat oven to 170°C/150°C fan-forced. Grease 19cm x 29cm slice pan; line with baking paper, extending paper 2cm over long sides.
2 Using fork, whisk egg whites in large bowl until combined. Add butter, milk, extract, ground almonds and sifted icing sugar and flour; stir until combined. Split vanilla bean in half lengthways; scrape seeds from bean, stir seeds into mixture.
3 Pour mixture into pan; sprinkle cherries over mixture.
4 Bake slice about 30 minutes. Stand slice in pan 10 minutes; turn, top-side up, onto wire rack to cool.

prep + cook time 55 minutes **makes** 16

rum and raisin chocolate slice

½ cup (75g) coarsely chopped raisins
2 tablespoons dark rum, warmed
150g milk eating chocolate, chopped coarsely
2 teaspoons vegetable oil
¼ cup (60ml) cream
200g dark eating chocolate, chopped coarsely

1 Combine raisins and rum in small bowl. Cover; stand 3 hours or overnight.
2 Grease 8cm x 25cm bar cake pan; line with foil, extending foil 5cm over two long sides.
3 Stir half the milk chocolate and half the oil in small heatproof bowl over small saucepan of simmering water until smooth; spread mixture over base of pan. Refrigerate about 10 minutes or until set.
4 Stir cream and dark chocolate in small saucepan over low heat until smooth. Stir in raisin mixture; spread over chocolate base. Refrigerate 20 minutes or until set.
5 Stir remaining milk chocolate and oil in small heatproof bowl over small saucepan of simmering water until smooth; spread over raisin mixture. Refrigerate 40 minutes or until set; remove from pan before cutting.

prep + cook time 35 minutes (+ standing & refrigeration) **makes** 12

triple choc brownies

125g butter, chopped
200g dark eating chocolate, chopped
½ cup (110g) caster sugar
2 eggs
1¼ cups (185g) plain flour
150g white eating chocolate, chopped
100g milk eating chocolate, chopped

1 Preheat oven to 180°C/160°C fan-forced. Grease deep 19cm-square cake pan; line with baking paper, extending paper 5cm over sides.
2 Stir butter and dark chocolate in medium saucepan over low heat until smooth. Cool 10 minutes.
3 Stir sugar and eggs into chocolate mixture, then sifted flour and white and milk chocolates. Spread mixture into pan.
4 Bake brownies about 35 minutes. Cool in pan.

prep + cook time 1 hour **makes** 16

fig and muscat brownies

½ cup (100g) finely chopped dried figs
¼ cup (60ml) muscat
125g butter, chopped coarsely
200g dark eating chocolate, chopped coarsely
⅔ cup (150g) caster sugar
2 eggs, beaten lightly
1¼ cups (185g) plain flour
150g dark eating chocolate, chopped coarsely, extra
1 tablespoon cocoa powder

1 Combine figs and muscat in small bowl; stand 20 minutes.
2 Preheat oven to 180°C/160°C fan-forced. Grease deep 19cm-square cake pan; line with baking paper, extending paper 5cm over sides.
3 Stir butter and chocolate in medium saucepan over low heat until smooth. Cool 10 minutes.
4 Stir sugar and eggs into chocolate mixture, then sifted flour, extra chocolate and fig mixture. Spread mixture into pan.
5 Bake brownies about 30 minutes. Cool in pan. Dust brownies with sifted cocoa; cut into squares.

prep + cook time 50 minutes (+ standing) **makes** 36

white chocolate, raspberry and macadamia blondies

125g butter, chopped
200g white eating chocolate
¾ cup (165g) caster sugar
2 eggs, beaten lightly
¾ cup (110g) plain flour
½ cup (75g) self-raising flour
100g white eating chocolate, chopped, extra
½ cup (75g) macadamias, roasted, chopped coarsely
150g fresh or frozen raspberries
1 tablespoon icing sugar

1 Preheat oven to 180°C/160°C fan-forced. Grease 23cm-square slab cake pan; line with baking paper extending paper 5cm over sides.
2 Stir butter and chocolate in medium saucepan over low heat, without boiling, until mixture is smooth. Cool until just warm.
3 Stir sugar and egg into chocolate mixture, then sifted flours, extra chocolate, nuts and raspberries. Spread mixture into pan.
4 Bake blondies about 40 minutes or until firm; cool in pan. Cut into nine squares; halve diagonally to form 18 triangles. Dust blondies with sifted icing sugar.

prep + cook time 55 minutes **makes** 18

chocolate fudge brownies

150g butter, chopped
300g dark eating chocolate, chopped
1½ cups (300g) firmly packed brown sugar
3 eggs, beaten lightly
2 teaspoons vanilla extract
¾ cup (110g) plain flour
¾ cup (140g) dark Choc Bits
½ cup (120g) sour cream
¾ cup (110g) macadamias, roasted, chopped coarsely
1 tablespoon cocoa powder

1 Preheat oven to 180°C/160°C fan-forced. Grease 19cm x 29cm rectangular slice pan; line base with baking paper extending paper 5cm over long sides.
2 Stir butter and chocolate in medium saucepan over low heat, without boiling, until mixture is smooth. Cool until just warm.
3 Stir sugar, egg and extract into chocolate mixture, then sifted flour, Choc Bits, cream and nuts. Spread mixture into pan.
4 Bake brownies about 40 minutes. Cover pan with foil; bake another 20 minutes. Cool in pan. Cut into 12 pieces; dust with sifted cocoa.

prep + cook time 55 minutes **makes** 12

cherry coconut brownies

125g butter, chopped
200g dark eating chocolate, chopped
1 cup (220g) caster sugar
2 eggs, beaten lightly
¾ cup (110g) plain flour
¼ cup (35g) self-raising flour
2 tablespoons cocoa powder
¼ cup (20g) desiccated coconut
85g Cherry Ripe chocolate bar, chopped
1 tablespoon cocoa powder, extra

1 Preheat oven to 180°C/160°C fan-forced. Grease 23cm-square slab cake pan; line with baking paper extending paper 5cm over sides.
2 Stir butter and chocolate in medium saucepan over low heat, without boiling, until mixture is smooth. Cool until just warm.
3 Stir sugar and egg into chocolate mixture, then combined sifted flours and cocoa, coconut and half the Cherry Ripe. Spread mixture into pan; top with remaining Cherry Ripe.
4 Bake brownies about 40 minutes; cool in pan. Cut into 24 pieces; dust with sifted extra cocoa.

prep + cook time 55 minutes **makes** 24

walnut brownie bites

½ cup (50g) walnuts, toasted, chopped finely
80g butter
150g dark eating chocolate, chopped coarsely
¾ cup (150g) firmly packed brown sugar
1 egg, beaten lightly
⅓ cup (50g) plain flour
¼ cup (60g) sour cream
3 x 50g packets Rolos

1 Preheat oven to 180°C/160°C fan-forced. Grease two 12-hole
(1½-tablespoon/30ml) mini muffin pans; divide walnuts among holes.
2 Stir butter and chocolate in small saucepan over low heat until smooth.
Stir in sugar; cool to just warm.
3 Stir egg into chocolate mixture, then sifted flour and sour cream.
Spoon mixture into pan holes; press a Rolo into centre of mixture,
spreading mixture so that Rolo is completely enclosed.
4 Bake bites about 15 minutes. Using a sharp-pointed knife, loosen
sides of brownies from pan holes; stand in pan 10 minutes. Remove
brownies gently from pan.

prep + cook time 35 minutes (+ standing) **makes** 24
tips Rolos are soft caramel-centred chocolates. They are available from
supermarkets. These bites are best served while still warm.

peanut butter brownies

180g butter, chopped
150g dark eating chocolate, chopped
1¾ cups (385g) caster sugar
4 eggs, beaten lightly
1 teaspoon vanilla extract
¾ cup (110g) plain flour
2 tablespoons self-raising flour
⅓ cup (35g) cocoa powder
50g dark eating chocolate, chopped, extra
⅓ cup (95g) crunchy peanut butter

1 Preheat oven to 180°C/160°C fan-forced. Grease 20cm x 30cm lamington pan; line with baking paper extending paper 5cm over long sides.
2 Stir butter and chocolate in medium saucepan over low heat, without boiling, until mixture is smooth; cool until just warm.
3 Stir sugar, egg and extract into chocolate mixture, then sifted flours, cocoa and extra chocolate. Pour mixture into pan. Drop small spoonfuls of peanut butter into chocolate mixture and swirl through with a knife.
4 Bake brownie about 50 minutes or until firm; cool in pan. Cut brownie into 24 pieces.

prep + cook time 1 hour 10 minutes **makes** 24

rocky road brownie slice

100g butter, chopped coarsely
200g dark eating chocolate, chopped coarsely
1 cup (220g) firmly packed brown sugar
2 eggs
½ cup (75g) plain flour
⅓ cup (80g) sour cream
200g toasted marshmallows, chopped coarsely
½ cup (70g) roasted slivered almonds
300g white eating chocolate, melted

1 Preheat oven to 180°C/160°C fan-forced. Grease 19cm x 30cm lamington pan; line with baking paper, extending paper 5cm over long sides.
2 Stir butter and dark chocolate in medium saucepan over low heat until smooth. Cool 10 minutes.
3 Stir sugar and eggs into chocolate mixture, then sifted flour and sour cream. Spread mixture into pan.
4 Bake slice about 35 minutes; cool in pan.
5 Combine marshmallows and nuts in medium bowl; sprinkle over slice, drizzle with white chocolate. Refrigerate until set.

prep + cook time 45 minutes (+ refrigeration) **makes** 30

PASTRIES

mini portuguese custard tarts

½ cup (110g) caster sugar
2 tablespoons cornflour
3 egg yolks
¾ cup (180ml) milk
½ cup (125ml) cream
1 vanilla bean
5cm strip lemon rind
1 sheet butter puff pastry

1 Preheat oven to 220°C/200°C fan-forced. Grease two 12-hole (1-tablespoon/20ml) mini muffin pans.
2 Combine sugar and cornflour in medium saucepan. Gradually whisk in combined egg yolks, milk and cream.
3 Split vanilla bean in half lengthways, scrape seeds into custard; add rind. Stir over medium heat until mixture just comes to the boil. Remove from heat; discard rind. Cover surface of custard with plastic wrap while making pastry cases.
4 Cut pastry sheet in half; stack halves, press firmly. Roll pastry up tightly from long side; cut log into 24 slices. Roll each pastry slice on floured surface into 6cm rounds; press rounds into pan holes. Pour custard into pastry cases.
5 Bake tarts about 12 minutes. Turn, top-side up, onto wire rack to cool. Serve dusted with a little sifted icing sugar.

prep + cook time 45 minutes (+ cooling) **makes** 24

brown sugar palmiers

1 cup (120g) pecans
⅓ cup (75g) firmly packed brown sugar
50g butter
1 teaspoon finely grated orange rind
1 sheet puff pastry
1 egg, beaten lightly

1 Preheat oven to 200°C/180°C fan-forced.
2 Process pecans, sugar, butter and rind until chopped finely.
3 Sprinkle pastry with half the nut mixture; fold two opposite sides of pastry inwards to meet in the centre. Flatten folded edges; brush with a little egg. Fold each side in half again to meet in the centre; flatten slightly and brush with egg. Fold two sides in half again to meet in the centre.
4 Repeat process with another pastry sheet, remaining nut mixture and egg. Enclose each log in plastic wrap; refrigerate 30 minutes.
5 Cut pastry into 1cm slices; place, cut-side up, on baking-paper-lined oven trays.
6 Bake palmiers about 15 minutes; cool on trays.

prep + cook time 35 minutes (+ refrigeration) **makes** 48

lemon meringue tartlets

4 egg yolks
⅓ cup (75g) caster sugar
2 teaspoons finely grated lemon rind
¼ cup (60ml) lemon juice
40g unsalted butter, chopped
24 x 4.5cm diameter baked pastry cases
meringue
1 egg white
¼ cup (55g) caster sugar

1 Stir egg yolks, sugar, rind, juice and butter in small heatproof bowl over small saucepan of simmering water until mixture thickens slightly and coats the back of a spoon. Remove pan from heat, remove bowl from pan immediately. Cover surface of lemon curd with plastic wrap; refrigerate until cold.
2 Preheat oven to 200°C/180°C fan-forced.
3 Meanwhile, make meringue.
4 Place pastry cases on oven tray; fill with curd, then top with meringue.
5 Bake tartlets about 5 minutes or until meringue is browned lightly.
meringue Beat egg white in small bowl with electric mixer until soft peaks form; gradually add sugar, beating until dissolved between additions.

prep + cook time 45 minutes (+ refrigeration) **makes** 24

coffee liqueur puffs

¼ cup (60ml) water
30g butter
¼ cup (35g) plain flour
1 egg, beaten lightly
1 tablespoon icing sugar
coffee liqueur cream
⅔ cup (160ml) thickened cream
1 tablespoon icing sugar
1 tablespoon coffee-flavoured liqueur

1 Preheat oven to 200°C/180°C fan-forced. Grease two oven trays.
2 Bring the water and butter to the boil in small saucepan; add sifted flour, stirring until mixture leaves side of pan. Remove pan from heat; cool 5 minutes.
3 Transfer mixture to small bowl; beat with electric mixer on medium speed. Gradually add egg, beating until mixture is glossy.
4 Spoon mixture into small piping bag fitted with 1.5cm plain tube. Pipe 2cm rounds, about 5cm apart, onto oven trays.
5 Bake puffs 10 minutes. Reduce oven to 180°C/160°C fan-forced; bake a further 20 minutes or until puffs are crisp.
6 Remove puffs from oven; make small slits in sides of each puff to let steam escape. Transfer puffs to wire rack to cool.
7 Meanwhile, make coffee liqueur cream.
8 Just before serving, spoon liqueur cream in small piping bag fitted with small plain tube. Make small hole in bottom of each puff; pipe cream into puffs. Dust with sifted icing sugar.
coffee liqueur cream Beat ingredients in small bowl with electric mixer until firm peaks form.

prep + cook time 1 hour (+ cooling) **makes** 15

chocolate custard tarts

3 egg yolks
½ cup (110g) caster sugar
2 tablespoons cornflour
1 tablespoon cocoa powder
¾ cup (180ml) milk
⅔ cup (160ml) cream
1 sheet puff pastry

1 Preheat oven to 220°C/200°C fan-forced. Grease two 12-hole (1-tablespoon/20ml) mini muffin pans.
2 Combine egg yolks, sugar, cornflour and cocoa in medium saucepan; whisk in milk and cream until smooth. Stir over heat until mixture boils and thickens; cool.
3 Cut pastry sheet in half; stack halves, press firmly. Roll pastry up tightly from long side; cut log into 24 slices. Roll slices between sheets of baking paper into 6cm rounds; press rounds into pan holes. Pour custard into pastry cases.
4 Bake tarts about 15 minutes. Cool in pan. Dust with sifted icing sugar, if you like.

prep + cook time 40 minutes **makes** 24

banoffee tartlets

395g can sweetened condensed milk
2 tablespoons golden syrup
60g unsalted butter
24 x 4.5cm diameter baked pastry cases
1 large banana (230g)
½ cup (125ml) thickened cream, whipped

1 Stir condensed milk, syrup and butter in small heavy-based saucepan over heat until smooth. Bring to the boil; boil, stirring, about 10 minutes or until thick and dark caramel in colour. Remove pan from heat; cool.
2 Spoon caramel into pastry cases; top with a slice of banana and a dollop of cream.

prep + cook time 30 minutes (+ cooling) **makes** 24

mini white chocolate and raspberry mille-feuilles

1 sheet puff pastry
50g white eating chocolate, melted
1 tablespoon raspberry jam
½ cup (125ml) thickened cream
50g white eating chocolate, grated finely
60g fresh raspberries
30g white eating chocolate, chopped coarsely
1 tablespoon thickened cream, extra
1 tablespoon icing sugar

1 Preheat oven to 240°C/220°C fan-forced. Grease oven tray.
2 Place pastry sheet on tray; place a second oven tray on top.
Bake about 15 minutes or until pastry is browned and crisp.
Cool 2 minutes.
3 Spread pastry with melted chocolate, then jam; cut into 18 rectangles.
4 Beat cream in small bowl with electric mixer until firm peaks form;
fold in grated chocolate.
5 Spread cream mixture over jam; sandwich pastry rectangles with
raspberries.
6 Stir chopped chocolate and extra cream in small heatproof bowl over
small saucepan of simmering water until smooth. Drizzle chocolate
mixture over mille-feuilles; dust with sifted icing sugar.

prep + cook time 40 minutes (+ cooling) **makes** 9

choc-topped zucotto

2 eggs
⅓ cup (75g) caster sugar
2 tablespoons cornflour
2 tablespoons plain flour
2 tablespoons self-raising flour
200g milk eating chocolate
2 tablespoons icing sugar
nutty cream
½ cup (125ml) thickened cream
1 tablespoon icing sugar
1 tablespoon hazelnut-flavoured liqueur
2 tablespoons finely chopped roasted hazelnuts
2 tablespoons finely chopped roasted almonds

1 Preheat oven to 180°C/160°C fan-forced. Grease and flour
three 12-hole shallow round-based patty pans.
2 Beat eggs in small bowl with electric mixer until thick and creamy.
Gradually add caster sugar, beating until sugar dissolves between
additions. Sift flours together three times; fold into egg mixture.
Drop rounded tablespoons of mixture into pans.
3 Bake cakes about 7 minutes; turn onto wire racks to cool.
4 Meanwhile, coarsely grate 1 tablespoon of chocolate from block of
chocolate; reserve grated chocolate. Melt remaining chocolate.
5 Make nutty cream.
6 Dip the knuckle of your index finger into icing sugar then use to
make a large hollow in the flat side of the cakes.
7 Spoon 1 teaspoon of the nutty cream into each hollow; smooth level.
Spread with melted chocolate. Set at room temperature.
8 Dust zucotto with sifted icing sugar to serve.
nutty cream Beat cream, sifted icing sugar and liqueur in small bowl
with electric mixer until firm peaks form. Stir in nuts and reserved
grated chocolate.

prep + cook time 45 minutes (+ cooling) **makes** 36

caramel cashew tarts

1 cup (150g) roasted
  unsalted cashews
1 tablespoon cornflour
¾ cup (165g) firmly packed
  brown sugar
2 tablespoons golden syrup
50g butter, melted
2 eggs
2 tablespoons cream
1 teaspoon vanilla extract

pastry
1¼ cups (185g) plain flour
¼ cup (55g) caster sugar
125g cold butter, chopped coarsely
1 egg yolk
2 teaspoons water
cinnamon cream
300ml thickened cream
1 tablespoon icing sugar
1 teaspoon ground cinnamon

1 Make pastry.
2 Grease two 12-hole (⅓-cup/80ml) muffin pans. Roll pastry between
sheets of baking paper to 3mm thickness; cut out twenty-four 8cm
rounds. Press rounds into pan holes; prick bases all over with fork.
Refrigerate 20 minutes.
3 Preheat oven to 200°C/180°C fan-forced.
4 Bake pastry cases 10 minutes. Cool.
5 Reduce oven to 160°C/140°C fan-forced.
6 Combine nuts and cornflour in medium bowl; stir in sugar, syrup,
butter, egg, cream and extract. Spoon mixture into pastry cases.
7 Bake tarts about 15 minutes; cool. Refrigerate 30 minutes.
8 Make cinnamon cream. Serve tarts with cream.
pastry Process flour, sugar and butter until coarse. Add egg yolk
and the water; process until combined. Knead on floured surface until
smooth. Cover; refrigerate 30 minutes.
cinnamon cream Beat ingredients in small bowl with electric mixer
until soft peaks form.

prep + cook time 45 minutes (+ refrigeration & cooling) **makes** 24

chocolate, quince and hazelnut tartlets

150g dark eating chocolate, chopped coarsely
⅓ cup (80ml) cream
40g unsalted butter
100g quince paste
¼ cup (35g) coarsely chopped roasted hazelnuts
pastry
¾ cup (110g) plain flour
¼ cup (25g) cocoa powder
¼ cup (40g) icing sugar
90g cold unsalted butter, chopped
1 egg yolk
1 tablespoon iced water, approximately

1 Make pastry.
2 Grease two 12-hole (1½-tablespoon/30ml) shallow round-based patty pans. Roll rounded teaspoons of pastry into balls, press over base and side of holes. Prick pastry all over with fork. Refrigerate 30 minutes.
3 Preheat oven to 180°C/160°C fan-forced.
4 Bake pastry cases 10 minutes.
5 Meanwhile, stir chocolate, cream and butter in small heatproof bowl over small saucepan of simmering water until smooth. Cool 15 minutes.
6 Soften paste in microwave oven on MEDIUM (75%) about 20 seconds.
7 Spoon paste into pastry cases; top with half of the nuts. Top with chocolate mixture, then remaining nuts. Refrigerate 1 hour.
pastry Process sifted flour, cocoa, icing sugar and butter until crumbly; add egg yolk and enough of the water, processing until ingredients just come together. Knead dough on floured surface until smooth. Enclose in plastic wrap; refrigerate 30 minutes.

prep + cook time 50 minutes (+ refrigeration & cooling) **makes** 24
tip Quince paste is available from delicatessens and most supermarkets, usually in the specialist cheese section.

fig baklava

1 cup (160g) roasted blanched almonds
1 cup (140g) roasted unsalted pistachios
1 cup (170g) coarsely chopped dried figs
2 teaspoons ground cinnamon
1 teaspoon ground clove
1 teaspoon ground nutmeg
9 sheets fillo pastry
80g butter, melted
honey syrup
1 cup (250ml) water
¾ cup (165g) caster sugar
⅓ cup (115g) honey
1 teaspoon finely grated lemon rind

1 Preheat oven to 200°C/180°C fan-forced. Grease deep 22cm-square cake pan.
2 Blend or process nuts, figs and spices until chopped finely.
3 Cut pastry sheets in half crossways. Layer three pastry squares, brushing each sheet with butter; place in pan, sprinkle with ½ cup of the nut mixture. Repeat layering with remaining pastry, butter and nut mixture, ending with pastry.
4 Cut baklava into quarters; cut each quarter into four triangles.
5 Bake baklava 25 minutes. Reduce oven to 150°C/130°C fan-forced; bake a further 10 minutes.
6 Meanwhile, stir ingredients for honey syrup in small saucepan over heat until sugar dissolves; bring to the boil. Reduce heat; simmer, uncovered, without stirring, 10 minutes.
7 Pour hot syrup over hot baklava; cool in pan.

prep + cook time 55 minutes **makes** 16

chocolate tarts

150g dark eating chocolate
¼ cup (60ml) thickened cream
1 tablespoon orange-flavoured liqueur
1 egg
2 egg yolks
2 tablespoons caster sugar
pastry
1⅔ cups (250g) plain flour
⅓ cup (75g) caster sugar
150g cold butter, chopped coarsely
1 egg yolk

1 Make pastry.
2 Grease two 12-hole (2-tablespoon/40ml) deep flat-based patty pans.
3 Roll pastry between sheets of baking paper to 3mm thickness; cut out twenty-four 6.5cm rounds. Press rounds into pan holes; prick bases all over with fork. Refrigerate 30 minutes.
4 Preheat oven to 200°C/180°C fan-forced.
5 Bake pastry cases 10 minutes. Cool.
6 Reduce oven to 180°C/160°C fan-forced.
7 Stir chocolate, cream and liqueur in small saucepan over low heat until smooth. Cool 5 minutes.
8 Meanwhile, beat egg, egg yolks and sugar in small bowl with electric mixer until light and fluffy; fold chocolate mixture into egg mixture. Spoon filling into pastry cases.
9 Bake tarts 8 minutes; cool 10 minutes. Refrigerate 1 hour. Serve dusted with a little sifted cocoa powder.
pastry Process flour, sugar and butter until coarse. Add egg yolk; process until combined. Knead pastry on floured surface until smooth. Cover; refrigerate 30 minutes.

prep + cook time 45 minutes (+ refrigeration & cooling) **makes** 24

sugary cinnamon twists

1 sheet puff pastry, thawed
20g butter, melted
2 tablespoons raw sugar
½ teaspoon ground cinnamon

1 Preheat oven to 200°C/180°C fan-forced. Grease two oven trays.
2 Brush pastry with butter; sprinkle with combined sugar and cinnamon.
Cut pastry in half. Turn one half over, sugar-side down; place the other
half, sugar-side up, on top. Press lightly to join layers. Cut pastry into
1cm-wide strips; twist each strip, then place on trays.
3 Bake twists about 10 minutes or until browned lightly and crisp;
transfer to wire rack to cool.

prep + cook time 20 minutes **makes** 25

pear frangipane galette

40g butter, softened
2 tablespoons caster sugar
1 egg yolk
½ cup (60g) ground almonds
1 tablespoon plain flour
1 sheet shortcrust pastry
1 medium corella pear (125g), unpeeled
2 tablespoons redcurrant jelly, warmed

1 Preheat oven to 220°C/200°C fan-forced. Line oven tray with baking paper.
2 Beat butter, sugar and egg yolk in small bowl with electric mixer until light and creamy. Stir in ground almonds and flour.
3 Cut pastry sheet into quarters; place on tray. Spread almond mixture onto pastry squares, leaving 2cm border. Arrange sliced pear on almond mixture; brush pear with jelly. Fold edges of pastry over to form a border.
4 Bake galettes about 15 minutes.

prep + cook time 45 minutes **makes** 4

palmiers with honey cream

2 tablespoons raw sugar
1 sheet puff pastry
1 teaspoon ground nutmeg
300ml thickened cream
2 teaspoons honey

1 Preheat oven to 180°C/160°C fan-forced. Grease two oven trays; line with baking paper.
2 Sprinkle board lightly with a little of the sugar. Roll pastry on sugared board into 20cm x 40cm rectangle; trim edges. Sprinkle pastry with nutmeg and remaining sugar.
3 Starting from long side, loosely roll one side at a time into the middle of the rectangle, so the two long sides meet in the centre. Cut pastry into 5mm-thick slices. Place, cut-side up, about 5cm apart, on trays. Spread pastry open slightly at folded ends to make a V-shape.
4 Bake palmiers about 15 minutes or until golden brown; transfer to wire rack to cool.
5 Beat cream and honey in small bowl with electric mixer until firm peaks form. Serve palmiers with honey cream.

prep + cook time 45 minutes **makes** 30

glossary

almonds flat, pointy-tipped nuts having a pitted brown shell enclosing a creamy white kernel which is covered by a brown skin.

flaked paper-thin slices.

ground also known as almond meal; nuts are powdered to a coarse flour texture for use in baking or as a thickening agent.

slivered small pieces cut lengthways.

baking powder a raising agent consisting mainly of two parts cream of tartar to one part bicarbonate of soda (baking soda).

basil, sweet the most common type of basil; used extensively in Italian dishes.

bicarbonate of soda also known as baking soda; a mild alkali used as a leavening agent in baking.

butter we use salted butter unless stated otherwise; 125g is equal to 1 stick (4oz) in other recipes. Unsalted or "sweet" butter has no added salt.

buttermilk originally the term given to the slightly sour liquid left after butter was churned from cream, today it is made similarly to yogurt. Sold alongside milk products in supermarkets. Despite the implication of its name, it is low in fat.

capers the grey-green buds of a warm climate (usually Mediterranean) shrub, sold either dried and salted or pickled in a vinegar brine; tiny young ones, called baby capers, are also available both in brine or dried in salt. Their pungent taste adds piquancy to a classic steak tartare, tapenade, sauces and condiments.

caraway seeds the small, half-moon-shaped dried seed from a member of the parsley family; adds a sharp anise flavour when used in sweet and savoury dishes. Used widely, in such different foods as rye bread, harissa and the classic Hungarian fresh cheese, liptauer.

cardamom a spice native to India and used extensively in its cuisine; can be purchased in pod, seed or ground form. Has a distinctive aromatic, sweetly rich flavour and is one of the world's most expensive spices. Used to flavour curries, rice dishes, sweet desserts and cakes.

cayenne pepper a thin-fleshed, long, extremely hot, dried red chilli, usually purchased ground.

cheese

blue vein mould-treated cheeses mottled with blue veining. Varieties include firm and crumbly stilton types and mild, creamy brie-like cheeses.

cream commonly known as philadelphia or philly; a soft cow-milk cheese with a fat content ranging from 14 to 33 per cent.

fetta Greek in origin; a crumbly textured goat- or sheep-milk cheese having a sharp, salty taste. Ripened and stored in salted whey; particularly good cubed and tossed into salads. We use a version having no more than 15 per cent fat when calling for low-fat cheese.

goat's made from goat milk, has an earthy, strong taste. Available in soft, crumbly and firm textures, in various shapes and sizes, and sometimes rolled in ash or herbs.

parmesan also called parmigiano, parmesan is a hard, grainy cow-milk cheese which originated in the Parma region of Italy. The curd for this cheese is salted in brine for a month before being aged for up to 2 years, preferably in humid conditions. Parmesan is grated or flaked and used for pasta, salads and soups; it is also eaten on its own with fruit. Reggiano is the best parmesan, aged for a minimum 2 years and made only in the Italian region of Emilia-Romagna.

ricotta a soft, sweet, moist, white cow-milk cheese with a low fat content (8.5 per cent) and a slightly grainy texture. Its name roughly translates as "cooked again" and refers to ricotta's manufacture from a whey that is itself a by-product of other cheese making.

chilli always use rubber gloves when seeding and chopping fresh chillies as they can burn your skin. We use unseeded chillies in our recipes because the seeds contain the heat; use fewer chillies rather than seeding the lot.

thai also known as "scuds"; tiny, very hot and bright red in colour.

chives related to the onion and leek; has a subtle onion flavour. Used more for flavour than as an ingredient.

chocolate

cherry ripe dark chocolate bar made with coconut and cherries; standard size bar weighs 55g.

Choc Bits also known as chocolate chips or chocolate morsels; available in milk, white and dark chocolate. Made of cocoa liquor, cocoa butter, sugar and an emulsifier; hold their shape in baking and are ideal for decorating.

dark eating also known as semi-sweet or luxury chocolate; made of a high percentage of cocoa liquor and cocoa butter, and little added sugar. Unless stated otherwise, we use dark eating chocolate in this book as it's ideal for use in desserts and cakes.

milk eating most popular eating chocolate, mild and very sweet; similar in make-up to dark with the difference being the addition of milk solids.

white eating contains no cocoa solids but derives its sweet flavour from cocoa butter. Very sensitive to heat.

chocolate hazelnut spread we use Nutella. It was originally developed when chocolate was hard to source during World War 2; hazelnuts were added to extend the chocolate supply.

cinnamon available in the piece (sticks or quills) and ground into powder; one of the world's most common spices, used universally as a flavouring for both sweet and savoury foods.

cloves dried flower buds of a tropical tree; can be used whole or in ground form. They have a strong scent and taste so should be used sparingly.

cocoa powder also known as unsweetened cocoa; cocoa beans (cacao seeds) that have been fermented, roasted, shelled, ground into powder then cleared of most of the fat content.

coconut

desiccated concentrated, dried, unsweetened and finely shredded coconut flesh.

flaked dried flaked coconut flesh.

shredded unsweetened thin strips of dried coconut flesh.

cornflour also called cornstarch. Available made from corn or wheat (wheaten cornflour, gluten-free, gives a lighter texture in cakes); used as a thickening agent in cooking.

cream of tartar the acid ingredient in baking powder; added to confectionery mixtures to help prevent sugar from crystallising. Keeps frostings creamy and improves volume when beating egg whites.

curry powder a blend of ground spices used for making Indian and some South East Asian

387

dishes. Consists of some of the following spices: cinnamon, dried chilli, coriander, cumin, fennel, fenugreek, mace, cardamom and turmeric. Available in mild or hot varieties.

custard powder instant mixture used to make pouring custard; similar to North American instant pudding mixes.

dried cranberries have the same slightly sour, succulent flavour as fresh cranberries. Can often be substituted for or with other dried fruit in most recipes. Available in most supermarkets.

dried currants dried tiny, almost black raisins so-named from the grape type native to Corinth, Greece; most often used in jams, jellies and sauces. These are not the same as fresh currants, which are the fruit of a plant in the gooseberry family.

eggs we use large chicken eggs (60g) in our recipes unless stated otherwise. If a recipe calls for raw or barely cooked eggs, exercise caution if there is a salmonella problem in your area.

essences are synthetically produced substances used in small amounts to impart their respective flavours to foods. An extract is made by actually extracting the flavour from a food product. In the case of vanilla, pods are soaked, usually in alcohol, to capture the authentic flavour. Both extracts and essences will keep indefinitely if stored in a cool dark place.

fennel seeds the name given to the dried seeds of the plant which have a strong licorice flavour.

figs fresh figs are best eaten in peak season, at the height of summer. They vary in skin and flesh colour according to type not ripeness. When ripe, figs should be unblemished and bursting with flesh; nectar beads at the base indicate when a fig is at its best.

five-spice although the ingredients vary from country to country, five-spice is usually a fragrant mixture of ground cinnamon, cloves, star anise, sichuan pepper and fennel seeds. Used in Chinese and other Asian cooking; available from most supermarkets or Asian food shops.

flour
plain also known as all-purpose; unbleached wheat flour is the best for baking.

rice very fine, almost powdery, gluten-free flour; made from ground white rice.

self-raising all-purpose plain or wholemeal flour with baking powder and salt added; can be made at home with plain or wholemeal flour sifted with baking powder in the proportion of 1 cup flour to 2 teaspoons baking powder.

wholemeal also called wholewheat flour; milled with the wheat germ so is higher in fibre and more nutritional than white flour. Available plain and self-raising.

food colouring vegetable-based substance available in liquid, paste or gel form.

fruit mince also called mincemeat. A mixture of dried fruits such as raisins, sultanas and candied peel, nuts, spices, apple, brandy or rum. Is used as a filling for cakes, puddings and fruit mince pies.

gelatine a thickening agent. Available in sheet form (leaf gelatine) or as a powder – 3 teaspoons powdered gelatine (8g or one sachet) is roughly equivalent to four gelatine leaves.

ginger
fresh also known as green or root ginger; the thick gnarled root of a tropical plant.

glacé fresh ginger root preserved in sugar syrup; crystallised ginger can be substituted if rinsed with warm water and dried before using.

ground also known as powdered ginger; used as a flavouring in cakes, pies and puddings but cannot be substituted for fresh ginger.

glacé fruit fruit such as pineapple, apricots, peaches and pears that are cooked in a heavy sugar syrup then dried.

glucose syrup also called liquid glucose, made from wheat starch; used in jam and confectionery making. Available at health-food stores and supermarkets.

golden syrup a by-product of refined sugarcane; pure maple syrup or honey can be substituted.

hazelnuts also called filberts; plump, grape-size, rich, sweet nut having a brown inedible skin that is removed by rubbing heated nuts together vigorously in a tea-towel.

ground is made by grounding the hazelnuts to a coarse flour texture.

honey honey sold in a squeezable container is not suitable for the recipes in this book.

jam also known as preserve or conserve.

jelly crystals a combination of sugar, gelatine, colours and flavours; when dissolved in water, the solution sets as firm jelly.

jersey caramels a softish confectionery, caramel in colour with a white stripe in the middle. Available in supermarkets.

liqueur
coconut-flavoured we use Malibu.

coffee-flavoured vodka or rum-based liqueur; we use Kahlua.

hazelnut-flavoured we use frangelico.

orange-flavoured brandy-based liqueur such as Grand Marnier or Cointreau.

macadamias native to Australia; fairly large, slightly soft, buttery rich nut. Should always be stored in the fridge to prevent their high oil content turning them rancid.

mandarin also known as tangerine; a small, loose-skinned, easy-to-peel, sweet and juicy citrus fruit, prized for its eating qualities more than for juicing. Segments in a light syrup are available canned.

maple-flavoured syrup is made from sugar cane and is also known as golden or pancake syrup. It is not a substitute for pure maple syrup.

maple syrup distilled from the sap of sugar maple trees found only in Canada and about ten states in the USA. Most often eaten with pancakes or waffles, but also used as an ingredient in baking or in preparing desserts. Maple-flavoured syrup or pancake syrup is not an adequate substitute for the real thing.

marzipan a paste made from ground almonds, sugar and water. Similar to almond paste but sweeter, more pliable and finer in texture. Easily coloured and rolled into thin sheets to cover cakes, or sculpted into shapes for confectionery.

milk we use full-cream homogenised milk unless stated otherwise.

evaporated unsweetened canned milk from which water has been extracted by evaporation. Evaporated skim or low-fat milk has 0.3 per cent fat content.

milk powder instant powdered milk made from cow's milk with liquid removed and emulsifiers added. Available in full-cream and skim varieties.

sweetened condensed a canned milk product consisting of milk with more than half the water content removed and sugar added to the remaining milk.

mixed peel candied citrus peel.

mixed spice a classic mixture generally containing caraway, allspice, coriander, cumin, nutmeg and ginger, although cinnamon and other spices can be added. It is used with fruit and in cakes.

nutmeg a strong and very pungent spice ground from the dried nut of an evergreen tree native to Indonesia. Usually found ground but the flavour is more intense from a whole nut, available from spice shops, so it's best to grate your own. Found in mixed spice mixtures.

oil

cooking spray we use a cholesterol-free cooking spray made from canola oil.

vegetable any oils sourced from plant rather than animal fats.

paprika ground dried sweet red capsicum (bell pepper); there are many grades and types available, including hot, sweet, mild and smoked.

parsley a versatile herb with a fresh, earthy flavour. There are about 30 varieties of curly parsley; the flat-leaf variety (continental or Italian parsley) is stronger in flavour and darker in colour.

pecans native to the US and now grown locally; pecans are golden brown, buttery and rich. Good in savoury as well as sweet dishes; walnuts are a good substitute.

pepitas the pale green kernels of dried pumpkin seeds; available plain or salted.

pine nuts also known as pignoli; not in fact a nut but a small, cream-coloured kernel from pine cones. They are best roasted before use to bring out the flavour.

pistachios green, delicately flavoured nuts inside hard off-white shells. Available salted or unsalted in their shells; you can also get them shelled.

polenta also known as cornmeal; a flour-like cereal made of dried corn (maize). Also the name of the dish made from it.

poppy seeds small, dried, bluish-grey seeds of the poppy plant, with a crunchy texture and a nutty flavour. Can be purchased whole or ground in most supermarkets.

prosciutto a kind of unsmoked Italian ham; salted, air-cured and aged, it is usually eaten uncooked.

raisins dried sweet grapes (traditionally muscatel grapes).

ready-made white icing also known as soft icing, ready-to-roll and prepared fondant. Available from the baking section in most supermarkets.

rhubarb classified as a vegetable, is eaten as a fruit and therefore considered one. Leaves must be removed before cooking as they can contain traces of poison; the edible crisp, pink-red stalks are chopped and cooked.

roasting/toasting nuts and dried coconut can be roasted in the oven to restore their fresh flavour and release their aromatic essential oils. Spread them evenly onto an oven tray then roast in a moderate oven for about 5 minutes. Desiccated coconut, pine nuts and sesame seeds roast more evenly if stirred over low heat in a heavy-based frying pan; their natural oils will help turn them golden brown.

rolled oats flattened oat grain rolled into flakes and traditionally used for porridge.

Instant oats are also available, but traditional oats are best for baking.

rosemary pungent herb with long, thin pointy leaves; use large and small sprigs, and the leaves are usually chopped finely.

rosewater extract made from crushed rose petals; used for its aromatic quality.

semolina coarsely ground flour milled from durum wheat; the flour used in making gnocchi, pasta and couscous.

sour cream thick, commercially-cultured sour cream with a minimum fat content of 35 per cent.

star anise a dried star-shaped pod whose seeds have an astringent aniseed flavour.

sugar we use coarse, granulated table sugar, also called crystal sugar, unless stated otherwise.

brown an extremely soft, fine granulated sugar retaining molasses for its characteristic colour and flavour.

caster also called superfine or finely granulated table sugar. The fine crystals dissolve easily so it is perfect for cakes, meringues and desserts.

demarara small-grained golden-coloured crystal sugar.

icing also known as confectioners' sugar or powdered sugar; pulverised granulated sugar crushed together with a small amount (about 3 per cent) of cornflour.

muscovado a fine-grained, moist sugar that comes in two types, light and dark. Light muscovado has a light toffee flavour and is good for sticky toffee sauce and caramel ice-cream. Dark muscovado is used in sweet and spicy sauces.

palm also called nam tan pip, jaggery, jawa or gula melaka; made from the sap of the sugar palm tree. Light brown to black in colour and usually sold in rock-hard cakes; use with brown sugar if unavailable.

pure icing also known as confectioners' sugar or powdered sugar.

raw natural brown granulated sugar.

tomatoes canned whole peeled tomatoes in natural juices; available crushed, chopped or diced. Use undrained.

paste triple-concentrated tomato puree used to flavour soups, stews, sauces and casseroles.

treacle thick, dark syrup not unlike molasses; a by-product of sugar refining.

vanilla

bean dried, long, thin pod from a tropical golden orchid grown in central and South America and Tahiti; the minuscule black seeds inside the bean are used to impart a luscious vanilla flavour in baking and desserts. Place a whole bean in a jar of sugar to make vanilla sugar.

extract obtained from vanilla beans infused in water; a non-alcoholic version of essence.

vinegar, malt made from fermented malt and beech shavings.

walnuts as well as being a good source of fibre and healthy oils, nuts contain a range of vitamins, minerals and other beneficial plant components called phytochemicals. Each type of nut has a special make-up and walnuts contain the beneficial omega-3 fatty acids, which is terrific news for people who dislike the taste of fish.

yeast (dried and fresh), a raising agent used in dough making. Granular (7g sachets) and fresh compressed (20g blocks) yeast can almost always be substituted one for the other when yeast is called for.

index

conversion chart

MEASURES

One Australian metric measuring cup holds approximately 250ml, one Australian metric tablespoon holds 20ml, one Australian metric teaspoon holds 5ml.

The difference between one country's measuring cups and another's is within a two- or three-teaspoon variance, and will not affect your cooking results.North America, New Zealand and the United Kingdom use a 15ml tablespoon.

All cup and spoon measurements are level. The most accurate way of measuring dry ingredients is to weigh them. When measuring liquids, use a clear glass or plastic jug with the metric markings.

We use large eggs with an average weight of 60g.

LIQUID MEASURES

METRIC	IMPERIAL
30ml	1 fluid oz
60ml	2 fluid oz
100ml	3 fluid oz
125ml	4 fluid oz
150ml	5 fluid oz (¼ pint/1 gill)
190ml	6 fluid oz
250ml	8 fluid oz
300ml	10 fluid oz (½ pint)
500ml	16 fluid oz
600ml	20 fluid oz (1 pint)
1000ml (1 litre)	1¾ pints

LENGTH MEASURES

METRIC	IMPERIAL
3mm	⅛in
6mm	¼in
1cm	½in
2cm	¾in
2.5cm	1in
5cm	2in
6cm	2½in
8cm	3in
10cm	4in
13cm	5in
15cm	6in
18cm	7in
20cm	8in
23cm	9in
25cm	10in
28cm	11in
30cm	12in (1ft)

DRY MEASURES

METRIC	IMPERIAL
15g	½oz
30g	1oz
60g	2oz
90g	3oz
125g	4oz (¼lb)
155g	5oz
185g	6oz
220g	7oz
250g	8oz (½lb)
280g	9oz
315g	10oz
345g	11oz
375g	12oz (¾lb)
410g	13oz
440g	14oz
470g	15oz
500g	16oz (1lb)
750g	24oz (1½lb)
1kg	32oz (2lb)

OVEN TEMPERATURES

The oven temperatures in this book are for conventional ovens;
if you have a fan-forced oven, decrease the temperature by 10-20 degrees.

	°C (CELSIUS)	°F (FAHRENHEIT)	GAS MARK
Very slow	120	250	½
Slow	150	300	1 – 2
Moderately slow	160	325	3
Moderate	180	350	4 – 5
Moderately hot	200	400	6
Hot	220	425	7 – 8
Very hot	240	475	9

Published in 2010 by ACP Books, Sydney
ACP Books are published by ACP Magazines, a division of PBL Media Pty Limited

ACP BOOKS

General manager Christine Whiston
Editor-in-chief Susan Tomnay
Creative director & designer Hieu Chi Nguyen
Art director Hannah Blackmore
Senior editor Stephanie Kistner
Food director Pamela Clark
Food editor Cathie Lonnie
Sales & rights director Brian Cearnes
Marketing manager Bridget Cody
Senior business analyst Rebecca Varela
Operations manager David Scotto
Production manager Victoria Jefferys

Published by ACP Books, a division of ACP Magazines Ltd.
54 Park St, Sydney NSW Australia 2000. GPO Box 4088, Sydney, NSW 2001.
Phone +61 2 9282 8618 Fax +61 2 9267 9438
acpbooks@acpmagazines.com.au www.acpbooks.com.au

Printed by Toppan Printing Co., China.

Australia Distributed by Network Services, GPO Box 4088, Sydney, NSW 2001.
Phone +61 2 9282 8777 Fax +61 2 9264 3278
networkweb@networkservicescompany.com.au
United Kingdom Distributed by Australian Consolidated Press (UK),
10 Scirocco Close, Moulton Park Office Village, Northampton, NN3 6AP.
Phone +44 1604 642 200 Fax +44 1604 642 300 .
books@acpuk.com www.acpuk.com
New Zealand Distributed by Southern Publishers Group, 21 Newton Road, Auckland.
Phone +64 9 360 0692 Fax +64 9 360 0695 hub@spg.co.nz
South Africa Distributed by PSD Promotions, 30 Diesel Road Isando, Gauteng Johannesburg.
PO Box 1175, Isando 1600, Gauteng Johannesburg.
Phone +27 11 392 6065/6/7 Fax +27 11 392 6079/80 orders@psdprom.co.za

Title: Biscuits/food director Pamela Clark
ISBN: 978-1-74245-001-8 (pbk)
Notes: Includes index.
Subjects: Cookies.
Other authors/contributors: Clark, Pamela
Dewey number: 641.8654
© ACP Magazines Ltd 2010
ABN 18 053 273 546

To order books, phone 136 116 (within Australia) or **order online** at www.acpbooks.com.au
Send recipe enquiries to: recipeenquiries@acpmagazines.com.au

Front cover & additional photography Julie Crespel
Front cover & additional styling Kate Nixon
Front cover & additional food preparation Sharon Kennedy